Twenty-First Century Poverty Trap

Twenty-First Century Poverty Trap

THE GREAT SOCIETY PROMISED
TO END POVERTY IN AMERICA.
HERE IS WHY IT DID NOT WORK,
AND HOW TO LAUNCH THE POOR
INTO MIDDLE INCOMES.

——◆——

James T. Moodey

THUNDER SOURCE PUBLISHING
CALIFORNIA

Published by,

Thunder Source Publishing
23325 Caminito Juanico
Laguna Hills, Ca. 92653

Format and printing by,
Create Space at Amazon

Back cover photo by Alan Root for National Geographic, 1973.
Taken on the Omo River in Ethiopia.
Courtesy of Alan Root.

Charts and related research are original, by the author.
ISBN-13: 9781523213665
ISBN-10: 1523213663

Also by James T. Moodey

Media Canards
Stunning stories the media hides from us.
IUniverse, publishers.

To my lovely daughter Claire, who I love more than all the stars, and to the good Lord who guides her. I pray that her generation can repair the problems that we, the baby boomers, created and save our poorest brethren.

Contents

Prologue

———————

DESPITE THE MANY TRILLIONS OF dollars Democrats have spent since Lyndon Johnson began the Great Society to end poverty in America, some Democrats are finally beginning to ask, "Why has the poverty rate *not* gone down?" This book will explain why.

Since Karl Marx published the *Communist Manifesto* and some of the Marx/Engels papers in 1848, the American media and many countries have been drawn to the ideal that socialism helps the poor. When implemented, the system rightly maintains the poor, but it creates additional poor people as well. In countries where socialism has been implemented in full, such as China and Russia, nearly everyone is poor. This book will explain the reason.

The answers to these questions begin with what made the United States different. It is that difference, that very attribute, that Democrats and socialists revile and destroy.

So what is that difference? What made us different? Why are America's poor wealthier than other poor people around the world? Why is our standard of living so much higher – what created America's tremendous wealth?

Let's begin there.

CHAPTER 1

How Did Capitalism in the U.S. Create So Much Wealth?

———◆———

What made our form of capitalism more successful than others?

WEALTH AND POVERTY DEFINED.

BEFORE WE CAN SOLVE ANY economic problem, we must identify the precise cause of the problem. Furthermore, to cure the economic problem of poverty, we must define wealth and poverty in real economic terms. Wealth should not be measured in currency. Currency can be inflated and is an astatic marker of wealth.

The wealth of a nation is its amount of usable goods, just as poverty is a lack of usable goods. Poverty in a society is created by a lack of clothes, food, vehicles, housing, etc. If the supply of these usable goods is low, naturally, there is not enough to go around. Obviously, this creates the divergence of wealthy and poor. It gets worse; those who *can* afford the limited supply of usable goods bid up the price, creating even more poor. A large supply of usable goods brings prices down so more people can afford them. As the supply of usable goods rises, poverty declines.

The United States grew to be wealthy because we created far more usable goods than other nations. But how did that happen?

ALL USABLE GOODS ARE CREATED BY MANUFACTURING – ALL OF THEM.

It is not the amount of money that manufacturing employees earn that is of value – it is the millions of shirts, hammers, and vaccines they produce that create wealth in a society. Farms and utilities may be included in the definition of manufacturers, whereby a small number of people produce food, water, gas, and electricity for millions. The question becomes, why did our factories produce so much more than other factories around the world?

Eighteenth century European farmers attached their failed machinery to a horse and pulled it to the smithy's forge for repair. Each part was hand forged and repaired. The process of building the machinery was slow and repairs were even slower. We inherited this slow process in the United States.

The reason our factories broke away from this low production manufacturing was the creative genius of our factory owners.

In 1793, Eli Whitney invented *milling machines* (a lathe and wire extruder) that produced *replaceable parts* for his cotton gin. Cloth for clothing had been scarce and affordable only to the wealthy because the green cotton seeds were sticky, not to mention painful, and they took time to clean. One cotton gin could clean as much cotton as fifty people.[1]

Whitney's factory was in New Haven, Connecticut, but the cotton gins were selling in the South. Replaceable parts made the cotton gins more practical. The serviceable cotton gins sold as fast as Whitney could produce them until Whitney's government patents failed him. Many people copied Whitney's cotton gin. Nevertheless, clothing in the U.S. became plentiful and the price came down significantly.

By the time Whitney died in 1825, the United States had become a producer of an annual 200 million pounds of cotton at an estimated 70 million dollars wealth of textiles and clothing.[2] In the South, millions of people benefited from jobs in many related endeavors.

A creator of useable goods creates jobs not only for his own enterprise, but also jobs for other enterprises. Other industries grew in addition

---

1 *World Book Encyclopedia;* Whitney, Eli.

2 *American Made;* third edition, page 27, by historian Harold C. Livesay.

to textile mills; such as, shipping to and from the mills, out of state and out of the country; seaports grew; manufacturing of clothing flourished, including dye and print shops; merchant shops expanded; construction jobs appeared nearly everywhere; sales jobs occurred at all levels of business; and land values tripled.[3]

Service sector jobs grew as well. Banks hired more loan officers and tellers to handle the loans and savings; law firms hired more lawyers to handle property transactions and contracts to prevent disputes; and insurance enterprises grew.

The terrible racism of slavery aside, jobs were created for millions and the work to produce cotton was made easier.

Whitney later perfected the use of replaceable parts with new types of milling machines to manufacture guns for the government. He created a new technical expertise, *mechanical engineering*, which led to the next generation's explosion of other manufacturing machines.

Eli Whitney

The high volume of cotton brought the price of clothing down so low that nearly everyone could afford it. It was Eli Whitney's genius that advanced the United States from wearing buckskins to clothing for the common man. Poverty began to decline.

———————❖———————

The next major step toward high production manufacturing was creation of the *distribution system* by Cyrus McCormick in about 1850. He had invented

---

3 Ibid. A judge's observation at the time, page 28.

the reaper in 1840, but there was an array of business problems that beset him. He was selling a complicated machine to farmers who did not understand it and were much less capable of its repair. Broken parts might cost the farmer his crop during the harvest. Further, banks would not loan to farmers and McCormick was stuck with farmer debt.[4] Sales and service were paramount and McCormick could not traverse the territory fast enough.

McCormick solved all of these problems by designing a unique system – a network of distributors with whom McCormick shared considerable profit. The distributors took over all sales and service. They stocked parts locally and performed repairs. Distributors henceforth took over the personal contact necessary to judge how creditworthy the farmers were and made the loans themselves. McCormick wisely turned farmers away form direct factory sales by telling them they had to buy from their respective distributor.[5]

Nearly everyone owned their own farm and there was a dire shortage of labor so wheat crops had commonly died in the field. Couples harvested what they could and carried it to market. By using the McCormick Reaper, farmers could harvest nearly three times the amount of wheat with much less effort.

Cyrus McCormick

Setting up distributors to profit by success of the reaper marked the next turning point in American business. Within just a few years, food and grain became plentiful and affordable. Thanks to the genius of Cyrus McCormick, food prices plunged so that nearly any American could afford it. The U.S. became the world's largest exporter of food. Poverty was declining still further.

---

4 Ibid, pages 49-51. Harold C. Lovesay's description of problems that beset McCormick.
5 Ibid, page 52. Paraphrasing Harold C. Lovesay's description of the first distribution system.

The American standard of living was rising rapidly while other countries could not figure how we did it. We didn't do it – so far, two men had done it – Eli Whitney and Cyrus McCormick. They would soon get help from hundreds of other factory owners.

McCormick's phenomenal success with his distribution system was copied by many local manufacturers. Soon these other factory owners carried McCormick's genius one step further. Distribution centers were given a wholesale price so they became profitable businesses, but factory owners added an additional discount and layer of profit to include retailers. This created a unique *three-tier-distribution system* (factory, distributor, and retailer). It worked well for *all* products, not just reapers. McCormick's exact system is used to this day by farm equipment and automobile manufacturers, but the three-tiered system created our enormous wholesale and retail trade industries.

Factory owners in the 1850s told distributors to set up retailers with discounts so they too could profit by selling the product. Distributors were also told to send any buyers back to the retailers. Because the distributor provided a nearby stock and a retail discount, retail stores became efficient and profitable businesses. Thereafter in the 1850s, retail stores appeared on nearly every street corner in America.

Prior to this, women made their own soap, household goods, clothes, and tended crops. Men planted crops, hand-forged steel tools, and built what they needed. Rather than make their own goods, people began to buy them at a local store. Rural couples were unshackled from the centuries old life of paupers.

The retail industry boomed, which created tremendous demand from retailers for new and more usable goods. Rural couples wanted more.

Our factory owners and CEOs have always been the cream that rises to the top of creativity and wealth creation for the masses, but here is where this early system gets so counterintuitive that many other nations still cannot figure it out.

Factory owners had wisely added another innovation of *factory recommended wholesale and retail prices*. The wisdom of this was to provide a structure of profits for all who sold their product. It might seem that factory recommended pricing would raise prices. If a widget is made for one dollar, why is it good, or fair, to sell it for a factory recommended price of six dollars? The resulting high volume of sales, however, creates an overwhelming larger drop in product cost. As the cost falls, the recommend pricing is reduced as well.

Say a girl sets up a stand to manufacture lemonade whereby the table, pitcher, and glasses cost $100. These are fixed costs. They do not vary with sales. Each lemon and sugar costs a dollar, and the number required varies with the number of sales. These are variable costs. If she only sells one lemonade, her cost per lemonade is $101. If she sells two, her cost per lemonade drops to $51.

Prices drop quickly with volume of sales. As sales volume rises, the fixed cost per product drops rapidly. As sales grow further, the factory makes better volume buys and variable costs begin to decline as well.

As sales grow, factories reduce prices to the distributors and the distributors reduce the price to retailers. Then, the factory adjusts down the factory recommended price to protect their sales volume from competitors.

Retail businesses thrived with the resulting reliable wholesale cost structure and factory recommended retail pricing. Retailers sold the product because they knew other retailers were receiving the same cost and no customer could go around them to buy from the factory or the distributor. The result was that both distributors and retailers felt safe to invest capital to open businesses, and to invest in sales forces, and to advertise.

———◆———

Manufacturing in the U.S. was set up to grow rapidly. Growth was only limited by the amount factories could produce.

Enter Andrew Carnegie. In 1865, Carnegie invested in several iron-works companies. He recognized the demand for steel from other factories and built his Pittsburg steel mill in 1873. At Carnegie Steel, he set up a double shift to produce steel 24/7 and provided incentives to the shift that produced the most. He began by walking the floor and paid his workers well. Production far exceeded other producers.

Andrew Carnegie

Over the next twenty-five years Carnegie Steel, alone, grew to exceed the total production of any country in Europe. His high production facility brought the price of steel down to about a fourth of its previous price.

Lower steel prices brought costs down for every product that contained steel. Hundreds of factory owners took advantage of the unrestricted supply of steel to supply our nation with everyday usable goods. With numerous factories producing high volume, the price of everyday usable goods dropped to within or near the budget of even the poorest American. Poverty was dropping still further.

As discussed, retail stores throughout America had been trying to supply ready-made goods to millions, and rural couples wanted more. Thanks to Andrew Carnegie and the many other factory owners of his time, our retail stores were able satisfy nearly every customer's demand.

Hundreds of factory owners throughout the rust belt were using steel and milling machines to make parts for more complex products.

Factory owners could conceive of almost any product that would be useful and ask their mechanical engineers to design and build it. The assembly of complex products however, took time and quality control was always a problem.

In 1909, Henry Ford added the innovation of an *assembly line* to increase production of his Model T cars. The lines used conveyors to bring the chassis and parts to the workers. The assembly line brought order to the installation of parts and each worker became expert at the installation of his part. This improved quality considerably. The Model T was long considered the most reliable car built.

More important, production increased from 12 ½ man-hours per car in 1912 to 1 ½ man-hours in 1914.[6] With fixed costs and increased production along with volume discounts of his variable costs, the cost per car plunged. The more he made, the lower the price. The price of Henry Ford's Model T fell from $850 to $260, putting the price well within reach of the average family.[7]

Given the average monthly wage of $55 at the time, this brought the standard of living up to the present day six months' wages to buy a low price new car ($260/$55=4.7 months to afford a new car).

How did this affect labor and employment?

Because sales volume was so high, Henry Ford was able to reduce prices *and increase wages*. He raised wages to $5 per day,[8] which was about 2 ¾ times the national average of $1.83 per day.[9] His distributors were able to do the same. Workers migrated from all over the country to work for Henry Ford.

Henry Ford, one man, employed 100,000 workers.[10] Untold wealth and jobs were created in related industries.

---

6   *World Book Encyclopedia;* Ford, Henry.

7   Ibid.

8   *American Made;* third edition, page 117, by Harold C. Lovesay.

9   *World Book Encyclopedia;* Ford, Henry.

10   From the *Ford Rouge Manufacturing Plant* factory tour literature.

The United States has consistently attained what is generally considered full employment at five percent unemployment, and our standard of living has been the highest in the world. This is a direct result of high volume manufacturing and the three-tier-distribution system wherein all three tiers of workers profit by selling the product.

So not only did high volume reduce the cost of usable goods, it

Henry Ford

made room for increased wages at all three levels of the distribution system. Our standard of living had risen faster than any nation. Prices were going down and wages were going up. Poverty had declined to approximate present day level.

The three-tier-distribution system that our factory owners created does not get enough credit for creating full employment. Imagine our three-tier-distribution system as a wide staircase with factories on the left, distributors in the center, and retailers on the right. People, *even with no education*, could enter the system in manufacturing, distribution, or retail and climb the stairs of pay scale. Elsewhere, people born poor would likely end up poor, as would their children. Not in the "land of opportunity," as foreigners named the United States.

Other societies did not catch on to the counterintuitive idea that the *higher price* of factory recommended pricing was the key to high volume; and therefore *lower prices* – not higher prices. Remember, it was the factory recommended pricing that *protected profits* of distributors and retailers, which led to the high volume of usable goods.

We don't hear much about factory recommended pricing anymore because it is so ingrained in our economic system. It has become a self-balancing system. If a customer inquires with a factory or distributor, they are referred to a retailer or sold at the retail price.

Many societies today, such as Middle Eastern societies, live in poverty because they won't buy the concept. In fact, these are barter societies, where the price that retailers charge is not protected by their suppliers – no prices are protected. The price structure collapses and high volume factories cannot survive. Without high volume factories the supply of usable goods is low; therefore, poverty remains high.

———•———

For a moment let's put the former description of high volume production and its benefit of lowering prices and poverty, in academic terms. It is called productivity. Economics professors throw this word around without fully understanding it; hence, this chapter explains it in real terms – not academic terms. In academia, productivity is generally described as production (GDP) divided by labor (workforce). They track the rate of increase in this formula.

A professor of economics at Princeton, Alan Binder, wrote in May 2015, "Are you worried about America's recent dismal productivity performance? You should be. I prefer to date the slowdown in productivity growth from the end of 2010 because productivity growth (non-farm) averaged a bountiful 2.6% per annum…but only a *paltry* .4% since. …the drop is large, and the scary thing is that we don't understand why."[11]

We certainly appreciate our professors for the practice and testing they give to our students, but academic economics is superficial analysis and not sufficient to solve real world problems. The axioms of supply and demand, and productivity, without real examples, are not sufficient to help us understand what we learned in this chapter.

The remainder of this book will attempt to explain why the Democrats have failed to reduce poverty using real world economic examples and offering solutions, rather than complaining and describing problems with economic formulas. The next chapter gives a private sector, real world, description of how Democrats are destroying factories.

---

11 *The Mystery of Declining Productivity Growth*; Wall Street Journal, May 15, 2015.

CHAPTER 2

The Devastation of Cap and Trade

———◆———

You didn't build that.

PRESIDENT OBAMA SAID IN 2012, "Somebody invested in roads and bridges. If you've got a business, you didn't build that. Somebody else made that happen." Our new Democrat leader, Elizabeth Warren, said essentially the same thing. This is economic stupidity. They actually believe this tripe. How do such sharp minds drift to the opposite of the truth?

Eli Whitney built his factory without the help of roads or bridges. Government roads and bridges didn't even exist. There were only walking paths and boats. Further, Whitney's government patent had so failed him that he refused to patent his invention of the milling machine and his many other inventions.[12]

As a matter of fact, the government didn't start asking for roads and bridges until after Henry Ford sold a Model T to nearly every family in America. It was Henry Ford's automobile that created the necessity for roads and bridges. The hundreds of aforementioned factory owners that built our nation's great wealth and made our workers the wealthiest in the world accomplished it without any help from government in any way. They only had horse trails.

---

12 *Encyclopedia Britannica*; 1995, Whitney, Eli.

The government doesn't build anything – they don't even build roads and bridges. Governments hire private sector contractors to build roads and bridges. The closest they come to producing wealth are public water districts. Even these water districts ask private contractors and engineers to bid the civil engineering, build the wells, the pipelines, the pumping stations – everything. NASA hires private sector contractors to build their rockets and satellites. The military hires private contractors. The Government doesn't build anything. They tax the private sector and then ask the private sector to build what the government wants.

The government does not build any useable goods. *The government does not create wealth.*

————◆————

We all recognize the need for government, to conceive of and allow us to vote for what the public wants for the common good. But Karl Marx and now the modern Democrats want something different. They want to level the play field. They revile the wealthy and large factories – the very ones that create the jobs, the wealth, and the usable goods that we all need.

Joseph Stalin went so far as to murder capitalists – some twenty million of them. He murdered and exiled private sector farmers that produced high volumes of food. What did he produce by replacing those private farmers with government run farms? Up until Perestroika in 1986, women stood in line at government food stores to buy bread made from wheat the U.S. sold to the Soviet government and a freeze-dried shrimp from Cuba. Most other food was sold in black markets. Some women resorted to prostitution to afford black market sundries and food. That is socialism. It creates shortages and poverty.

Democrats may say they don't revile and destroy our factories, but their actions belie their words. They tax our corporations at the highest total tax rates in the world – to the point that, recently, many large factories are leaving the United States. For those that stay, the economic environment is becoming destructive.

The cap-and-trade rule in the Los Angeles basin caused over 1,200 of the approximate 1,800 factories to close and sell their machinery to Chinese manufactures. They are still closing. Let's look at this real life example before we get back to Karl Marx and the Democrats.

CAP AND TRADE.

How do I know 1,200 factories closed and sold their machinery to Chinese manufacturers? I counted them – right out of my own company database. My company was the sole source for gas physics compliance testing to comply with the original cap-and-trade rule, RECLAIM and rule 1146, implemented on January 1, 1994 by the South Coast Air Quality District (SCAQMD). The rule was later renamed cap and trade.

California had already established the Air Resources Board (ARB) with jurisdiction over *smog emitting cars and trucks*. Then the national air quality rule authorized states to enforce their own rules. What a mistake that was.

The California legislature established the nation's first air quality district, the SCAQMD, with authority over the entire Los Angeles metropolitan area and jurisdiction over everything except cars and trucks – everything *except smog*.

At first they didn't seem to know what to regulate; but, apparently they knew they had better stay away from regulating residences. Naturally, they started writing rules to regulate factories. Just like homeowners factories only have two sources of energy, electricity and clean burning natural gas. Black inky smoke does not come from factories – it comes from vehicles.

Factory owners were already buying instruments and hiring our company for anything to do with gas physics and gas measurement. One of our divisions repaired and distributed gas instruments and the other was a California Weights and Measures test facility for industrial applications. Other, government owned, Weights and Measures test facilities had jurisdiction over residential submetering and gasoline pump station accuracy. We were a private facility that handled everything else, *and we were busy*.

In retrospect, I realize we were busy because gas physics training and education is skipped over by our universities. They do a good job teaching engineering and physics but gas physics has been advanced far beyond what is taught in universities. Professors teach one hundred to three hundred year old gas physics theories that, when tested in real world applications, proved to be false or not usable.

Engineers at our factories, who design and build gas physics instruments, began disproving what was taught by academia as early as 1860. Our universities never got the memo. Students from our universities had to ignore what they had been taught. We taught them, and sent them to be taught by factory engineers. More detail about this is written in Chapter Nine.

SCAQMD wrote 1,145 rules prior to the cap-and-trade rule, all without higher authority or oversight by the legislature. They could write any laws they liked and were granted police power to enforce them. They hired young university graduates who wrote many compliance citations up to $5,000. Our factory owners were paralyzed with fear.

One factory owner muttered, "The SCAQMD has turned into a big fee machine." Many of the early rules required permits with annual fees for anything that used natural gas, oil, starch, glue or anything that smelled (which they called volatile organic compounds, VOCs), including the smell from bakeries.

Residences in the basin burn over 200 times more natural gas than factories, but the air quality district knew regulating residences would be political suicide.

Then, in 1992-4, they wrote what the factory owners had heard about and feared most, rule 1146 and RECLAIM (later renamed cap and trade).

The by-products of natural gas combustion are .9994 carbon dioxide and water vapor, which the district knew were harmless molecules. At the time they had not thought to demonize carbon dioxide. That happened after they got away with the following canard. The district determined that trace molecules of nitrogen can be found in natural gas. These too are harmless, but the public didn't generally know that.

So the district mandated the reduction of the trace amounts of nitrogen molecules, which they nicknamed NOx, from the exhaust of natural gas. All of the NOx molecules combined comprise less than 1 part per 1,700 in the exhaust of natural gas.[13] All of the molecules in the exhaust of natural gas are harmless – *we breathe them over our natural gas ranges in the kitchen.* The district was seeking a solution for a problem that did not exist.

The *first* list of companies required to comply consisted of our largest 466 factories, including a handful of utilities. The rule required an average 75 percent reduction over five years. In the week of January 1, 1994, when the rule was implemented, eight factories announced that they would close. If you were a factory owner that had plotted a 5 percent growth plan to keep up with competition, what would you do if a law landed on your desk mandating a 20 percent *annual reduction* in your only production heat source?

Factories that were able to reduce gas below their assigned targets could sell energy credits to the SCAQMD, who brokered them to factories that could not meet their targeted reductions. The credits were called Reclaim Trading Credits (RTCs). The cost of RTCs increased from zero cost in 1995; to $154 in 1996; $227 in 1997; $451 in 1998; $4,284 in 1999; $15,377 in 2000; and to $62,000 in 2001.[14]

Prices were driven up, naturally, by demand for a shrinking supply of credits. Many factories were closing by this time, so the SCAQMD removed the utilities from the rule to reduce the price of RTCs. Environmentalists complained that removing the largest users defeated the purpose of the rule; but much economic damage had already been done, and is still being done because the rule has been reapplied to smaller and smaller factories.

Factories were closing not only because of the high cost of RTCs, but because of the required reduction of their production. They were being

---

13 Calculated from a table in the Energy Information Administration, *Natural Gas* 1998: Issues and Trends, pg 58.

14 *An overview of the regional clean air initiatives market (RECLAIM) staff paper;* by the SCAQMD, Aug 14, 2006, pages 7&8.

forced to produce less each year while their competitors around the world were growing. Productivity was beginning to drop.

By the SCAQMD's own count in 2004, there were only 311 factories left in the large factory group, down from the original 466.[15] That was just the list of the very largest factories. They had gone on to reapply the rule to smaller factories.

To meet the approximate 20 percent reduction in year two, almost all factories replaced their burners with low temperature burners, at about $35,000 per boiler (boilers are large water heaters). In year three, many decided to shut down boiler #4, for example. The hand writing was there for them to see and factories were closing throughout the term of the rule. This affected all types of factories that use natural gas including bakeries.

When the rule began, it applied only to factories with heat equipment at 10,000,000 BTU's or more (the list of 466). As we approached the end of the five years, in 1998, the SCAQMD decided to add a new list of smaller factories using 5,000,000 BTU equipment. This, ostensibly, was to extend careers of the nearly 800 people at the air quality district. They never stopped. Eventually they lowered the compliance threshold all the way down to 75,000 BTUs (residential size) – the smallest of factories. This chart shows the reductions.

Chinese entrepreneurs were the only outsiders smart enough to recognize what was happening. They were aware of our factory closings because they have always had numerous import/export individuals here to buy for Chinese buyers; parts, equipment, or other needed items. The Chinese observed our factories closing and began to make offers for the manufacturing equipment.

Kaiser Steel's Fontana, California plant number one foundry was the first to go. The Chinese buyers leased an old motel in San Bernardino for about a year to house their workers. They built a fence around the

---

15 The 311 number is from the March 2, 2007 SCAQMD board meeting agenda no. 34, "The RECLAIM universe consisted of 311 facilities at the end of 2004." The 466 total is from the SCAQMD's *RECLAIM NOx Universe of Sources Draft List*, 3/31/93.

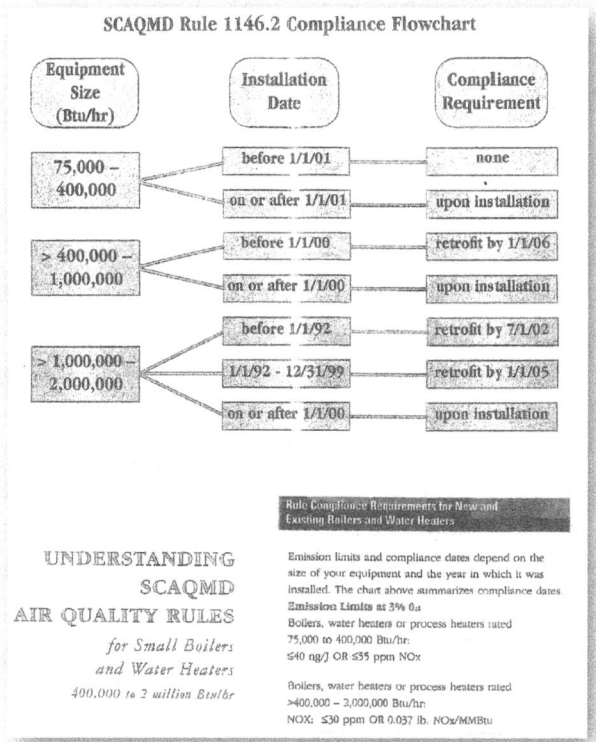

SCAQMD Rule 1146.2 Compliance Flowchart

Equipment Size (Btu/hr)	Installation Date	Compliance Requirement
75,000 – 400,000	before 1/1/01	none
	on or after 1/1/01	upon installation
> 400,000 – 1,000,000	before 1/1/00	retrofit by 1/1/06
	on or after 1/1/00	upon installation
> 1,000,000 – 2,000,000	before 1/1/92	retrofit by 7/1/02
	1/1/92 - 12/31/99	retrofit by 1/1/05
	on or after 1/1/00	upon installation

Rule Compliance Requirements for New and Existing Boilers and Water Heaters

UNDERSTANDING SCAQMD AIR QUALITY RULES

for Small Boilers and Water Heaters

400,000 to 2 million Btu/hr

Emission limits and compliance dates depend on the size of your equipment and the year in which it was installed. The chart above summarizes compliance dates.

Emission Limits at 3% O₂

Boilers, water heaters or process heaters rated 75,000 to 400,000 Btu/hr:
≤40 ng/J OR ≤35 ppm NOx

Boilers, water heaters or process heaters rated >400,000 – 2,000,000 Btu/hr:
NOX: ≤30 ppm OR 0.037 lb. NOx/MMBtu

*Southern California Gas Company information
brochure sent to their factory customers.*

motel and bought an old bus that took them to the Kaiser site every day. They painted what looked like white numbers on each piece of equipment including every girder, tin metal wall, nut, and bolt so the equipment and old building could be precisely rebuilt. Then they disassembled the metal building as well as the furnaces. It looked like a scrap metal heap for months. Slowly the pile of scrap disappeared as if removed by ants. Henry Kaiser's original foundry that got us through World War II and beyond was gone forever – never to be rebuilt or replaced.

Most factories tried to hang on while they made other plans; but in the end, almost all of them simply closed and sold their machinery to Chinese import/export representatives.

None of them exported jobs to China. That was an assumption and a media canard made by Thomas Friedman of the New York Times. Oh sure, some in the telecommunications industry hire overseas. They are not factories. Factories do not hire people elsewhere (except sales people) when the machinery is here. The factories simply closed and laid off their employees.

Chinese factory owners were anxious to export to the U.S. and what better plan was there than to buy the very machinery to make what Americans were already buying. The Los Angeles basin had been the largest manufacturing market in the country. The cap-and-trade rule was the very reason we now buy so much from China.

By the time I sold the interest in my company and quit counting, 1,210 of the approximate 1,800 factories in the Los Angeles basin had closed. Donald Sachs, Executive Director of the City of Industry Manufacturer's Council and Chamber of Commerce, said in 2008, "Eighty percent of our factories in the City of Industry have closed in the last fifteen years."

———————

Democrats were so inspired by their success of regulating NOx at our factories that they decided maybe they could get away with regulating the other remaining molecule of natural gas exhaust that they originally had declared to be harmless, carbon dioxide.

They proudly sell cap and trade as their ingenious free market approach to induce factories to voluntarily reduce their emissions. There is nothing voluntary about it.

They copied the SCAQMD rule into Waxman-Markey HR2454, but this time they got caught. Every single Republican in the Senate voted against it and it sits at the EPA waiting for a second chance. On page 683, the bill requires an 83 percent reduction – even more devastating than the 75 percent reduction of the Los Angeles rule and, this time, it will be nationwide.

MARX AND THE DEMOCRATS.

Notice that Democrats blamed factories (big business) when cars and trucks are the cause of smog. Yes, smog levels have improved, but that is almost entirely due to the use of catalytic converters – the invention of an oil refinery engineer.

They couldn't stand that their rule was stopped in the Senate, so they took their case to the Supreme Court. The Supreme Court unwittingly approved a most devastating rule when they gave the EPA authority to regulate carbon dioxide.

Democrats in the know are very aware of the devastation that the Los Angeles rule caused. They have been told over and over. The reality is, they simply don't care. They have been told by *real* scientists that carbon dioxide levels don't comport with temperature – they don't care.

I say Democrats here, rather than scientists. There is a reason. They are political advocates. The real scientists are skeptical. These skeptical scientists meet at the Climate Change Conference to express their skepticism about global warming theories. This is not publicized by our leftist media.

Some of these scientists are, Richard Lindzen, Ph.D., with degrees in physics and mathematics from Harvard University and Sloan Professor of atmospheric sciences emeritus at M.I.T.; Habibulo Abdussamatov, Dr.Sci., degree in astrophysics from the Russian Academy of Sciences; Robert M. Carter, Ph.D., degrees in geology and paleo- ecology from University of Otego, New Zealand; Ian Plimer, Ph.D., doctorate of geology from Macquarie University, Australia; Fred Singer, Ph.D., degree in atmospheric science and doctorate of meteorology from University of Wisconsin; Patrick Moore, Ph.D., (*Co-founder of Greenpeace*) doctorate of ecology at University of British Columbia; Arthur Robinson Ph.D., degrees in chemistry and biochemistry from Caltech and University of California San Diego.

Dr. Robinson circulated a petition to scientists to stop the Kyoto Protocol, which is the international version of cap and trade. The petition was eventually signed by thousands of scientists who identified themselves as professors of atmospheric, environmental, earth sciences, physics, and aerospace sciences.

The opposing force is led by the Union of Concerned Scientists (UCS). Past president of the Union of Concerned Scientists was Kevin Knobloch who has a B.S. in *journalism* and an M.S. in *public administration.* He was followed by, Kathleen Rest with an M.S in *public administration* and a Ph.D. in *health policy.* The current president is Kenneth Kimmell who has a *law degree.* The Director of Science, Peter Frumhoff has a B.A. in *psychology* and a Ph.D. in *ecology* with experience being a professor of *environmental law* at Fletcher School of Law and *professor of diplomacy* at Tufts University, Harvard and University of Maryland. The director of strategy is Alden Myer who has a B.S. in *political science* and an M.S. in *human resources.* Beneath Mr. Myer are *media director,* Elliott Negin and four *press secretaries.*[16]

That is the Union of Concerned Scientists. *These are not scientists;* they are political advocates – essentially, Democrats.

So how are Democrats led away from science into political advocacy? It was James Hansen, the man who coined the term global warming. According to Mitch Battros of *Earth Changes Media,* there is an old Washington Post story titled, *U.S. Scientist Sees New Ice Age Coming,* published July 9, 1971. He said, "It told of a prediction by scientists James Hansen and S.I. Rasool of Columbia University, stating the coming ice age is caused by human pollutants."

Then Hansen flip-flopped to scare us about warming in 1988 when temperatures began to rise. Hansen testified before Al Gore's committee and the media spread the fear.

Since that time Democrats, led by Al Gore, have appropriated federal funding of $22.5 billion per year to study global warming. It seems our

---

16 From the Union of Concerned Scientists web site 2008, and the current web site.

universities and their professors don't care about the truth of this subject. What they do care about is funding.

By the Democrats own numbers, carbon dioxide levels grew at their fastest rate during the post war boom from 1945 to 1978, while temperatures cooled. And now the same is happening again. For eighteen years, by the Democrat's own numbers, there has been no warming while carbon dioxide levels are rising.

There is overwhelming proof that carbon dioxide does not cause warming in the atmosphere, but – they don't care.

Why don't Democrats care? For the same reason Karl Marx wouldn't care – they are ideologues. Their ideology is that factories (big businesses) are evil and may be put down by whatever means available. If there are no truthful means to put factories down, they will make one up.

"factories of death"

- James Hansen

CHAPTER 3

Why Democrats Can't Solve Economic Problems

———◆———

Becoming liberal is an epiphany, becoming conservative
is a learning process.

IDEOLOGUES CAN'T SOLVE ECONOMIC PROBLEMS. Why? Because their ideology predetermines who is to blame. There is an even more specific answer.

In nearly all of the economic problems of our day, there is one common thread – Democrats cannot, or will not, *identify the true cause* of an economic problem. As mentioned, the Democrat's cap-and-trade rule blames factories (big business), when cars and trucks are the cause of smog.

This is the reason they have not solved the very problems that they care so much about. When a private sector CEO has a problem, he seeks the precise cause and corrects it. Democrats have predetermined causes that do not change because of their ideology. The result is an ever-growing system wherein problems are almost never solved, even as they throw more and more money at them.

———◆———

Let's consider the original question in the book's prologue: Despite the many trillions of dollars Democrats have spent since they began their

Great Society to end poverty in America, why has the poverty rate not gone down? Just as any CEO would do, let's identify the precise cause and begin by considering the largest demographic of chronic poverty.

Without getting lost in numbers, it should be obvious that millions of seniors trying to live on a median Social Security pension that *pays below the poverty level* for a senior couple is a good place to start.[17] Eighty-two percent of our population will be dependant upon Social Security, and half of the pensions pay below the poverty level for an elderly couple ($14,309 per year)!

The high Social Security-Medicare annual income tax of 15.3 percent and the low poverty level payout are the primary reason the poverty level has not decreased since the Great Society promised to end poverty. Social Security is not saving seniors – it is taking most of their spendable income and locking them into a poverty trap.

That much money (15.3 percent) taxed annually – whether some of it is a tax on the worker through the employer or not – nearly destroys the worker's ability to save and invest on his own. Then, the low pension payback locks the pensioner into or near poverty upon retirement. Nearly a sixth of all seniors are chronically impoverished in the United States. Even those who are paid above the poverty level are still paid close to it.

This writer, who kept and rented his first condominium, has been a landlord since 1976. In the early years, almost all of the tenant inquiries were from young couples. Now, the most recent tenant rollover produced only one out of eleven inquiries from young people. Ten inquiries were from seniors trying to rent. This was somewhat of an anomaly, but the trend is noticeable and significant. *Seniors are not being saved by Social Security, they are devastated by it.*

This is the largest demographic of chronic poverty and, yet, it is the easiest problem to solve.

The cause of the problem is that private sector workers' ownership of their pension money is taken from them, and it is not invested so it does not compound. The proper solution – to privatize the retirement funds – would

17 Pension Rights Center quoting Social Security Administration median pension at $14,093 and the U.S. Census Bureau Poverty Threshold for senior couples at $14,309.

take a CEO a few days to solve. The time for Democrats to solve the problem has been nearly eighty years and counting. Why can't they solve this very simple economic problem? Because they cannot and will not, identify the true *cause* of the economic problem.

The Democrat ideology predetermines who is to blame and it is nearly always the same – the evil Republicans or evil big business. Both these notions are the opposite of the truth. This, by the way, is the reason we have polar opposite viewpoints on so many subjects.

Republicans are the ones who understand how the economy works and are trying to repair economic problems. Big business is the reason our nation is wealthy and it is the job creator. The Democrat ideology, led by their media, seeks to destroy both. Take it from a 1960s leftist war protester turned conservative, becoming liberal is an epiphany, becoming conservative is a learning process.

We pick on Democrats for good reason. Social Security is their program. They completely control it and won't let Republicans do anything to change it – except raise taxes. George W. Bush called for ideas on how to at least partially privatize Social Security. He chose the only Democrat proposal, which increased payments to the poor at a greater rate with a small portion available to invest in a private account so it would earn a return. President Bush hoped, by choosing the Democrat proposal, it had a chance. He said his economic council advisor was told by a senior Democrat, "... our leaders have made clear we're not supposed to cooperate."[18]

When Milton Friedman proposed to Jimmy Carter that we privatize Social Security-Medicare, Carter ignored him. When Ronald Reagan proposed to privatize Social Security-Medicare, Tip O'Neill thundered almost daily, for weeks, into media microphones set up on the steps of Congress, "Reagan is just trying to line the pockets of his rich friends on Wall Street." When George W. Bush tried to at least partially privatize Social Security-Medicare, the left-wing media ranted, "We can't, they will lose all their money in the stock market." When Paul Ryan tried,

---

18 *Decision Points*; by George W. Bush, page 300.

Democrats ran a television ad showing Republicans pushing an old lady in a wheelchair off a cliff.

Once again, the common thread of Democrat ideology: Big business and Republicans are evil.

———◆———

In the next chapter, we will answer a question that no one has asked, "What *would* have happened if we had privatized Social Security?"

That would be the first question a CEO would ask. The answer is staggering – over half of private sector pensioners would now be millionaires and those that were not, would be close to it. Millions of chronically impoverished Americans would drop off the poverty roles. Let's take a look.

CHAPTER 4

The Largest Cause of Chronic Poverty is Social Security

It's not saving seniors – it's locking them into poverty.

THIS CHAPTER ANSWERS THE OVERWHELMINGLY obvious question that no one has asked, "What *would* have happened had we privatized Social Security?" The answer is staggering.

Privately invested large cap mutual funds typically track with growth of the Dow Jones Averages. This chapter lists the actual Dow Averages over the past to determine how much our Social Security funds would have grown, had they been invested.

A simple spreadsheet (See following page, Exhibit 1) tracking actual Dow Jones Averages proves that, had we privatized Social Security, a person with a taxable income beginning at $12,020 per year to $46,420 at age 65, *would have retired with about $1,015,300* in their Social Security account. This includes all the downturns including the 2008 downturn (a worst-case example).

The second page of Exhibit 1 shows the retirement years. The declining balance of savings at an annual return of 5 percent would then provide that pensioner a *retirement income of $80,027 per year* until the money ran out at age 85.

With $80,027 per year, retirees could pay for a $20,000 per year private medical policy thereby eliminating the need for Medicare. The retiree would still have $60,000 per year to age 85. What does this retiree receive now from Social Security? The answer is about $10,775 per year – well below poverty level.

Exhibit 2 shows what would have happened if a pensioner retired in 2014 when the stock market was higher. *The result is staggering – those with a lifetime average taxable income of only $19,846 would be millionaires.*

Please take time to review the charts carefully (Exhibits 1 & 2). They are easy to understand. Each example has two sections, a time period during working years that accumulates the money and a time period of retirement when the money is spent.

Exhibit 1 shows a beginning taxable income of $12,020 per year at age 21 in the left column. The right column shows the accumulating wealth of the invested proceeds using the *actual* Dow Jones Averages. The second page of Exhibit 1 shows the retirement years starting at age 65 when the pensioner has accumulated $1,015,300. The right column shows the annual retirement amount of $80,027 per year to age 85.

These numbers are only disputable in minor increments.[19] The examples are very conservative since the life expectancy is to about age 80, not 85. The numbers are even more conservative in that they assume we do not shift our money into money market funds during the downturns.

---

19 The chart uses current tax rates. If we plug in the lower tax rates in the early years, the pension in the first example for the low-income individual is still high at $54,131 per year. Since tax rates are not going to go down, it is relevant to estimate future results by using current rates.

Twenty-First Century Poverty Trap

EXHIBIT 1 – RETIRED IN 2008

YOUR ANNUAL RETIREMENT INCOME HAD YOUR LIFETIME ANNUAL EARNINGS GROWN FROM $12,020 TO $46,420: $80,027

YEAR	AGE	TAXED INCOME	SOCIAL SECURITY TOTAL TAX	END DOW JONES AVERAGE	COMPOUND BALANCE INVESTED
1963				766	
1964	21	$12,020	$1,839	874	$2,098
1965	22	$13,823	$2,115	969	$4,671
1966	23	$15,896	$2,432	786	$5,762
1967	24	$18,281	$2,797	906	$9,866
1968	25	$21,023	$3,217	948	$13,689
1969	26	$21,444	$3,281	809	$14,481
1970	27	$21,872	$3,346	839	$18,489
1971	28	$22,310	$3,413	890	$23,234
1972	29	$22,756	$3,482	1,032	$30,978
1973	30	$23,211	$3,551	855	$28,607
1974	31	$23,675	$3,622	632	$23,823
1975	32	$24,149	$3,695	852	$37,097
1976	33	$24,632	$3,769	1,005	$48,204
1977	34	$25,124	$3,844	831	$43,037
1978	35	$25,627	$3,921	805	$45,489
1979	36	$26,140	$3,999	839	$51,578
1980	37	$26,662	$4,079	964	$63,950
1981	38	$27,196	$4,161	875	$61,823
1982	39	$27,739	$4,244	1,047	$79,054
1983	40	$28,294	$4,329	1,259	$100,266
1984	41	$28,860	$4,416	1,212	$100,774
1985	42	$29,437	$4,504	1,546	$134,290
1986	43	$30,026	$4,594	1,896	$170,326
1987	44	$30,627	$4,686	1,939	$178,981

YEAR	AGE	TAXED INCOME	SOCIAL SECURITY TOTAL TAX	END DOW JONES AVERAGE	COMPOUND BALANCE INVESTED
1988	45	$31,239	$4,780	2,169	$205,558
1989	46	$31,864	$4,875	2,753	$267,092
1990	47	$32,501	$4,973	2,634	$260,304
1991	48	$33,151	$5,072	3,169	$319,278
1992	49	$33,814	$5,174	3,301	$337,966
1993	50	$34,491	$5,277	3,754	$390,347
1994	51	$35,180	$5,383	3,834	$404,163
1995	52	$35,884	$5,490	5,117	$546,738
1996	53	$36,602	$5,600	6,448	$696,008
1997	54	$37,334	$5,712	7,908	$860,609
1998	55	$38,080	$5,826	9,181	$1,005,911
1999	56	$38,842	$5,943	11,497	$1,267,104
2000	57	$39,619	$6,062	10,788	$1,194,652
2001	58	$40,411	$6,183	10,022	$1,115,569
2002	59	$41,219	$6,307	8,342	$933,815
2003	60	$42,044	$6,433	10,454	$1,178,296
2004	61	$42,885	$6,561	10,783	$1,222,146
2005	62	$43,742	$6,693	10,718	$1,221,431
2006	63	$44,617	$6,826	12,463	$1,428,231
2007	64	$45,510	$6,963	13,265	$1,527,549
2008	65	$46,420	$7,102	8,776	**$1,015,311**
TOTAL INVESTED:			$210,570		

AVG. INCOME: **$30,584**

EXHIBIT 1 (Continued)

UNDER THE CURRENT SYSTEM, YOU WOULD RECEIVE APPROXIMATELY:				HAD WE PRIVATIZED SOCIAL SECURITY, YOU WOULD RECEIVE:	
YEAR	AGE	SOC. SEC. INCOME/YR	VS.	INVESTED PROCEEDS	TOTAL INCOME/YR
2009	66	$10,775		$1,015,311	$80,027
2010	67	$10,937		$982,048	$80,027
2011	68	$11,101		$947,123	$80,027
2012	69	$11,267		$910,451	$80,027
2013	70	$11,436		$871,945	$80,027
2014	71	$11,608		$831,514	$80,027
2015	72	$11,782		$789,062	$80,027
2016	73	$11,959		$744,487	$80,027
2017	74	$12,138		$697,683	$80,027
2018	75	$12,320		$648,539	$80,027
2019	76	$12,505		$596,937	$80,027
2020	77	$12,692		$542,756	$80,027
2021	78	$12,883		$485,866	$80,027
2022	79	$13,076		$426,131	$80,027
2023	80	$13,272		$363,409	$80,027
2024	81	$13,471		$297,552	$80,027
2025	82	$13,673		$228,401	$80,027
2026	83	$13,878		$155,793	$80,027
2027	84	$14,087		$79,555	$80,027
2028	85	$14,298		-$496	$80,027

NOTES:
1. Assumed compound growth rate during retirement is 0.05 percent – a safety balanced portfolio.
2. On the previous page, the earnings growth rate decreases to 2 percent after the first five years.
3. On the previous page, the Social Security tax is combined contributions of employer and employee.

EXHIBIT 2 – RETIRED IN 2014

YOUR ANNUAL RETIREMENT INCOME HAD YOUR LIFETIME ANNUAL EARNINGS GROWN FROM $7,800 TO $30,123: $79,051

YEAR	AGE	TAXED INCOME	SOCIAL SECURITY TOTAL TAX	END DOW JONES AVERAGE	COMPOUND BALANCE INVESTED
1969				809	
1970	21	$7,800	$1,193	839	$1,238
1971	22	$8,970	$1,372	890	$2,769
1972	23	$10,316	$1,578	1,032	$5,041
1973	24	$11,863	$1,815	855	$5,680
1974	25	$13,642	$2,087	632	$5,741
1975	26	$13,915	$2,129	852	$10,610
1976	27	$14,193	$2,172	1,005	$15,077
1977	28	$14,477	$2,215	831	$14,298
1978	29	$14,767	$2,259	805	$16,039
1979	30	$15,062	$2,305	839	$19,119
1980	31	$15,363	$2,351	964	$24,668
1981	32	$15,671	$2,398	875	$24,567
1982	33	$15,984	$2,446	1,047	$32,322
1983	34	$16,304	$2,494	1,259	$41,866
1984	35	$16,630	$2,544	1,212	$42,753
1985	36	$16,962	$2,595	1,546	$57,845
1986	37	$17,302	$2,647	1,896	$74,187
1987	38	$17,648	$2,700	1,939	$78,631
1988	39	$18,001	$2,754	2,169	$91,038
1989	40	$18,361	$2,809	2,753	$119,116
1990	41	$18,728	$2,865	2,634	$116,708
1991	42	$19,102	$2,923	3,169	$143,930
1992	43	$19,484	$2,981	3,301	$153,030

YEAR	AGE	TAXED INCOME	SOCIAL SECURITY TOTAL TAX	END DOW JONES AVERAGE	COMPOUND BALANCE INVESTED
1993	44	$19,874	$3,041	3,754	$177,489
1994	45	$20,272	$3,102	3,834	$184,439
1995	46	$20,677	$3,164	5,117	$250,381
1996	47	$21,091	$3,227	6,448	$319,575
1997	48	$21,512	$3,291	7,908	$395,972
1998	49	$21,943	$3,357	9,181	$463,612
1999	50	$22,382	$3,424	11,497	$584,851
2000	51	$22,829	$3,493	10,788	$552,062
2001	52	$23,286	$3,563	10,022	$516,172
2002	53	$23,751	$3,634	8,342	$432,671
2003	54	$24,227	$3,707	10,454	$546,858
2004	55	$24,711	$3,781	10,783	$567,968
2005	56	$25,205	$3,856	10,718	$568,377
2006	57	$25,709	$3,934	12,463	$665,489
2007	58	$26,224	$4,012	13,265	$712,584
2008	59	$26,748	$4,092	8,776	$474,146
2009	60	$27,283	$4,174	10,428	$568,360
2010	61	$27,829	$4,258	11,578	$635,766
2011	62	$28,385	$4,343	12,218	$675,492
2012	63	$28,953	$4,430	13,104	$729,227
2013	64	$29,532	$4,518	16,577	$928,213
2014	65	$30,123	$4,609	17,823	**$1,002,937**
TOTAL INVESTED:			$136,643		
AVG. INCOME:		**$19,846**			

EXHIBIT 2 (Continued)

UNDER THE CURRENT SYSTEM, YOU WOULD RECEIVE APPROXIMATELY:

HAD WE PRIVATIZED SOCIAL SECURITY, YOU WOULD RECEIVE:

YEAR	AGE	SOC. SEC. INCOME/YR	VS.	INVESTED PROCEEDS	TOTAL INCOME/YR
2015	66	$9,095		$1,002,937	$79,051
2016	67	$9,231		$970,080	$79,051
2017	68	$9,370		$935,580	$79,051
2018	69	$9,510		$899,354	$79,051
2019	70	$9,653		$861,318	$79,051
2020	71	$9,798		$821,380	$79,051
2021	72	$9,945		$779,445	$79,051
2022	73	$10,094		$735,413	$79,051
2023	74	$10,245		$689,180	$79,051
2024	75	$10,399		$640,635	$79,051
2025	76	$10,555		$589,662	$79,051
2026	77	$10,713		$536,141	$79,051
2027	78	$10,874		$479,944	$79,051
2028	79	$11,037		$420,938	$79,051
2029	80	$11,203		$358,980	$79,051
2030	81	$11,371		$293,925	$79,051
2031	82	$11,541		$225,618	$79,051
2032	83	$11,715		$153,894	$79,051
2033	84	$11,890		$78,585	$79,051
2034	85	$12,069		-$490	$79,051

NOTES:

1. Assumed compound growth rate during retirement is 0.05 percent – a safety balanced portfolio.

2. On the previous page, the earnings growth rate decreases to 2 percent after the first five years.

3. On the previous page, the Social Security tax is combined contributions of employer and employee.

We have all heard the investment advice that if we saved and invested ten percent of our earnings every year, we would end up millionaires. Social Security-Medicare taxes our income 15.3 percent. It does not matter that some of it is contributed by our employer, it is for *our* retirement. As proven by the first chart, 15.3 percent invested compounds to make even a low-income earner into a millionaire.

A proper application of Social Security privatization would treat the account like 401(k) and IRA accounts. The new account would be self managed just like 401(k)s. Rules are already in place for the proper management of these funds. There would be no noticeable difference to the worker, except that his Social Security contribution begins accumulating in his own private account. There is no impact to the employer, because the company continues to make the same contribution to the worker's Social Security account.

For employers privatization would be a push – *for workers it would be a life-changing advantage.*

The existing notion that the Social Security account is not touchable until retirement is a good one. This prevents us from withdrawing our retirement early, or with a penalty. The government determined retirement age (62 and 65) could start getting younger instead of older since the retirement funds would accumulate at a high rate. Eventually, the 15.3% tax rate could be reduced.

The accumulated funds would be more than enough to also privatize and eliminate Medicare. This change would be phased in over time. The retiree would have plenty of money to pay for his own private medical insurance. Medicare doctors are being paid less and less. Services are declining and will only get worse.

As we gradually privatize, the federal stress of both entitlement programs would be removed from the budget. The pensioner would have about seven to nine times as much money to easily cover medical insurance and they would receive better care.

The affect of privatization on the economy would be positive since the amount Congress keeps and does not pay to retirees would be invested in the private sector instead of the government.

A close look at the exhibits reveals it is not true that during the downturns we will lose our money. Notice that the accumulating investment grows back quickly after the downturns.

This brings us to the real reason privatization of Social Security-Medicare is such a good idea. Let's compare the rising ups and downs of a privatized account versus a Social Security account. When you pay into your Social Security account, the principal balance goes poof and it is gone. That's right, what you invest is given to others and any excess not paid to others is spent by Congress. Your Social Security-Medicare principal balance drops to zero every year.

Think about it this way. Imagine you have two different mutual funds. The first is called LF (Legitimate Fund). In the first year you invest $1,000. During the next year, the market goes down 20 percent so you have $800 and in the second year you invest another $1,000 so you now have $1,800. Simultaneously you invested in your other fund, SSF (Social Security Fund). Your first year $1,000 goes poof and then your second year $1,000 goes poof and you have a zero balance. So even though the market crashed 20 percent, you are far better off having invested in the Legitimate Fund.

It does not matter that the market goes up and down. What matters is that your principal is invested and it is yours. The government can't take it and spend it as they are doing now. Aside from that, the invested funds *do* grow over time. That lost 20 percent grows back quickly, and then some.

Democrats and their media that tell us, "We can't privatize because the retirees will lose all their money," are on the opposite side of the truth. We lose our money when we put it in Social Security. They will say, "But the government will pay you and they really care." Take a look at the exhibits again. They show a side by side comparison of the actual private returns and what Social Security actually pays us. The exhibits prove them wrong. The truth is – they *don't* care.

In May 1980, the Chilean government privatized their retirement system after Milton Friedman first proposed it. It worked similar to what
these numbers suggest it would. José Piñera, the then Minister of Labor
states,

> "Chile's private pension system has been the main factor in increas-
> ing the savings rate to the level of an Asian tiger. Our rate is 26
> percent of GNP, compared to about 15 percent in Latin America…
> Pension reform has contributed strongly to an increase in the rate
> of economic growth. Before the 1970s Chile had a real growth
> rate of 3.5 percent. For the last 10 years we have been growing at
> the rate of 7 percent, double our historic rate. That is the most
> powerful means of eliminating poverty because growth increases
> employment and wages. Several experts have attributed the dou-
> bling of the growth rate to the private pension system."[20]

So Señior Piñera observed that the entire economy benefited due to the
large increase in savings rate. A high savings rate in the private sector is
beneficial because it increases capital investment which creates products
and jobs.

The Chileans began by offering a choice to workers of the new privatized retirement system or the existing government system, which was a
copy of our Social Security system. Roughly half of the workers did not
trust the private sector and opted for the government run system. Within
the first two years, nearly all of them scrambled to get into the privatized
system. Señior Piñera further states,

> "Ninety percent of Chile's workers chose to move into the new
> system. We have calculated that the typical Chilean worker's main

---

20 CATO Policy Reports, *The Success of Chile's Privatized Social Security*, by José Piñera,
former Minister of Labor and Current President of the International Center for Pension
Reform.

asset is not his small house or his used car but the capital in his pension account."[21]

Investors Business Daily reported that, "The Chilean poverty rate dropped from 45 percent to 15 percent and per capita annual income is up from $1,400 in 1986 to $15,000 by 2009." That is a 66 percent drop in poverty rate.

Every American, particularly young ones, should review these exhibits. Why won't they? The media won't publish such proof because it supports a Republican idea. Meanwhile many of our elderly, having invested enough of their hard earned dollars into the Social Security system to be millionaires, live in poverty.

---

21 Ibid.

CHAPTER 5

Why Hasn't the Poverty Rate Gone Down?

———◆———

Here is what we can do to correct the problem.

As THE PREVIOUS CHAPTER MADE clear, had we privatized Social Security, nearly all private sector pensioners would have been lifted into middle and upper incomes upon retirement. Most certainly the poverty rate would have declined, and it is easily quantified.

Had we privatized Social Security, 5.9 million seniors would be lifted off the U.S. Census supplemental measure of poverty roles and *the poverty rate would have dropped 15 percent by 2006* (from 12.3 percent to 10.4 percent). Subsequently, the poverty rate rose to 15.0 percent during the financial crisis, which we will discuss in Chapter Seven.[22]

Not only would the poverty rate have declined by 15 percent, nineteen million private sector pensioners who are poor and at risk of poverty (200 percent of the supplemental poverty level) would have gained substantial financial wealth. According to the most recent U.S. Census, *48 percent of all private sector seniors are in that demographic of poor.*[23] *All* of them would rise to middle or upper income upon retirement. Currently these seniors are dropping into poverty as their savings run out.

---

22 From U.S. Census numbers in 2006 and 2014.

23 *A State-by-State Snapshot of Poverty among Seniors: Findings From Analysis of the Supplemental Poverty Measure*; May 20, 2013, by the Henry Kaiser Family Foundation.

No CEO would bother to pinpoint these numbers or predict the exact result. Since the cause of the economic problem is so obvious, he would simply fix it. He would fix it quickly and move on to the next problem.

But how would he fix it? It is seemingly an enormous problem. No it isn't, it is a very simple economic problem. Before we get to that, there are several imagined complexities about doing this.

First, there is an *imagined* decline in the birth rate after the baby boomers whereby there are not enough young people to carry the burden. Yes the birth rate surged after World War II, but it has remained high and only decreased slowly over the years. There are plenty of young people paying in.

Second, public sector workers say, "We have privatized pension funds and we are way underfunded." Yes they are underfunded, but that is because they pay too little in and ask for too much out. The actual contribution of a teacher until recently (before some limited reforms) has been fairly typical. The contribution to retirement, right off her pay stub, was $50. She was paid monthly, but only for ten months of the year. That was a $500 contribution from her annual $93,000 salary. That is about one half of one percent (.5 percent), *thirty times less contribution than a private sector worker* (15.3 percent). Further, the payout pensions are *seven to nine times larger* than Social Security. There is no need to finish the math of *that* unfairness. Still further, the invested money for public workers *has* compound seven to nine times what was invested over the last forty-five years. The former charts prove that.

Another imagined complexity is by some Republicans, "The added weight on the stock market will depress stocks and that will be self defeating." The total market capitalization of the American stock markets is approximately $53 trillion dollars. Social Security will add about 1.4 percent. The invested capital of all 401(k) money is $2.5 trillion according to the Investment Company Institute. That is almost four times the capital absorption required to privatize Social Security.

When the Chileans transitioned to a private system, their problem was relatively small. They were able to finance the transition by selling government bonds and it happened rather quickly. Had we done this when

Milton Friedman first recommended it, our transition would have happened rather quickly. Now the problem is bigger, but the math is the same. It will simply take longer for the transition to complete.

If we make the transition formula flexible as to length of time, we reduce the problems of stress on the treasury and any slow growth in the economy. Having crunched the numbers, a reasonable guess might be fifteen to twenty years.

That is not too long to assure our youth that they will retire as millionaires or close to it. This includes all private sector workers *including our minorities*, many of whom fear that they have no hope of financial security. It will also provide our youth a tremendous incentive to work. The more they work, the faster their pension will grow, and they will *see* it growing.

Presently, the vast majority of private sector workers have to work until they die. Our youth recognize this and commonly say, "Social Security won't be there for us." Unfortunately, they are right to be discouraged. Democrats can't recognize the cause of the problem; meanwhile, it is the most significant problem facing private sector workers in our country.

Let's fix the problem. Focus on the cause: *The Social Security-Medicare pensioner has no legal right to his pension funds, which are not invested and do not compound.*

In 1968, Democrats voted themselves the right to take excess Social Security tax proceeds and put them into the general fund to spend. This abhorrent theft of our pension money would land anyone from the private sector in jail. They replace the stolen money with debt instruments that they call, "special issue U.S. Government securities." Following is a statement from the *Official Social Security Website*, in their own words, trying to make this sound good:

> "Tax income is deposited on a daily basis and is invested in "special-issue" securities. The cash exchanged for the securities goes into the general fund of the Treasury and is indistinguishable from other cash in the general fund. Money flowing into the trust funds is invested in U. S. Government securities. Because the government spends this borrowed cash, some people see the trust fund

assets as an accumulation of securities that the government will be unable to make good on in the future. Without legislation to restore long-range solvency of the trust funds, redemption of long-term securities prior to maturity would be necessary. Far from being worthless IOUs, the investments held by the trust funds are backed by the full faith and credit of the U. S. Government."

They *are* worthless IOUs because they are never sold for cash. They are probably not even marketable as is. And we *don't* trust the full faith and credit of Democrats who have spent all of the pension money leaving us with a reported fifteen trillion dollar liability to future pensioners, plus the excess tax revenues over what they paid to pensioners of two and one-half trillion dollars. They even admit they can't pay it back when they say, "Without legislation to restore long-range solvency of the trust funds, redemption of long-term securities prior to maturity would be necessary." Their solution is, give us more money.

Democrats are using your pension money as a revenue source by spending the excess of what they take in over the amount they pay to pensioners. They are so desperate for tax dollars that they tax you on these funds twice. They tax you on the money before you pay it to them; then, if your income is above twenty-five thousand dollars when you receive it as a pensioner, they tax you again.

So the principal you invested over the years is gone. There is no cash in your account – you don't even have an account. Even if there were cash, Democrats have made it abundantly clear in two court cases, that it is not your money – it is theirs. It is the government's money. *You need to own this money so they can no longer spend it.*

FOUR WAYS WE CAN FINANCE THE CONVERSION TO PRIVATE ACCOUNTS.

There are a number of methods to finance the transition. We must provide financing to maintain pensions for existing and future pensioners while we transition young workers into private accounts. This can be done on a sliding scale so middle age and even older workers can participate, at least to some extent, in the private sector growth. The amount that we transition young people away from paying into Social Security is the amount of financing required.

Even though all our pension money *is lost*, there is a solution. That two and one-half trillion dollars of "special issue U.S. Government securities" (worthless IOUs) represents the excess tax proceeds over what they have paid to pensioners that have accumulated over forty-six years. This means they have taxed an average of about 15 percent more per year than what they paid out.[24]

This amount of excess tax dollars should be used as the first source of financing to transition into private accounts. So we keep the 15.3 percent tax coming in and about 15 percent of that, rather than being spent by the government, is used to fund the annual transition. On average this is about $110 billion per year. This amount of excess taxes varies up and down with the economy and Medicare expense, but it does not matter – use whatever is there each year.

The transition process can and should be accelerated further by a second financing method of actually redeeming (selling) the "special issue government securities." As is, they are not marketable. They would have to be converted into real government treasury bonds and sold in the open market, whereby foreign investors can help fund our retirement. In other words, we should make the Democrats pay back the two and one-half trillion dollars that they skimmed off the top from our retirement contributions.

Spread out over a transition period of fifteen years, these treasury bonds would provide another $166 billion of annual financing. Together with the fluctuating $110 billion of excess Social Security tax revenues that are no longer spent by congress, the total financing might average around $276 billion per year. This should be called "equitable financing"

---

24 The calculation is, divide $2.5 trillion by 46 years equals $54 billion per year divided by $350 billion approximate average payout to seniors equals about 15 percent.

because *all of it* is the pensioner's money that has been taken from them. It is only equitable that it should apply to their retirement.

A third form of equitable financing to accelerate the transition can come from the pensioners themselves. Notice in the retirement portion of Exhibits 1 and 2 in Chapter Four, the *privatized funds grew about seven to nine times faster* than Social Security ($80,027/yr. vs. $10,775/yr. and $79,051/yr. vs. $9,095/yr.). As the Chileans discovered and our youth will quickly discover, the privatized portion of their retirement money will grow about eight times faster than the Social Security portion. Our government can simply include a provision in the transition formula that any worker can accelerate his transition into privatized funds by paying extra Social Security taxes. This will add a logarithmic acceleration to the transition time.

A fourth form of financing is always available – selling non-equitable government bonds on the open market. This can and should be done to reduce poverty and assist our seniors by attracting funds from local and foreign investors. This was the Chilean method.

ACCORDING TO THE CHILEANS, THE TRANSITION TO PRIVATIZED RETIREMENT WILL CREATE FOUR DIFFERENT EFFECTS THAT LOWER THE POVERTY RATE.

1) With the pension increase, six million seniors will drop off the poverty roles. As determined, this will reduce the poverty rate 15 percent. Furthermore, millions who are just above the poverty rate will *not* drop into poverty when their savings run dry.

2) Workers have more incentive to work since they can see their pensions grow quickly with their efforts. This produces more participation in the workforce. In addition, incomes accelerate due to the added incentive – they work harder.

3) The savings rate in the U.S. will rise rapidly. The higher savings rate, which represents invested capital in the economy, doubled

the Chilean economy's growth rate. Their minister of labor spe-
cifically credited the accelerated growth rate with new job creation and the reduction of their poverty rate from 45 percent to
15 percent.

4) The saved pension money is private and the excess will be inherited by the pensioner's children, adding financial wealth from generation to generation.

The latter three effects will reduce poverty beyond the 15 percent
drop produced by item one. The Chileans reduced their poverty rate 66
percent by privatizing their Social Security, which was a copy of ours.
*Given the analysis herein and the real results in Chile, the U.S. poverty rate
will drop somewhere between 15 percent and 66 percent if we privatize Social
Security.*

———◆———

The mood of our private sector workers is dismal. Most of them go to work
every day knowing they will likely have to work until they die. Politicians
and government workers have no idea what a depressing, sick feeling that
gives to our workers. Don't we owe them more than that? Where is the
feeling and caring?

Meanwhile, Chilean grandparents are happily retired, shopping in
malls to buy gifts for their grandchildren.

CHAPTER 6

What Else Can We Do To Reduce Poverty?

———◆———

Let's repair regulations that cause it.

ANOTHER COMMONLY MENTIONED DEMOGRAPHIC OF chronic poverty is broken families. Broken families and Social Security are the twin pillars of wealth destruction that are causing poverty in America.

When the Great Society began, Democrat Daniel Patrick Moynihan became Assistant Secretary of Labor. He conducted a study and wrote a report in 1965 that became known as the *Moynihan Report*. It pointed out that family structure in our African-American urban centers had become unstable. His comments were criticized by the left-wing of his party as racist. At the time, African Americans had a slightly higher than normal incidence of fatherless families of about 25 percent. Then the Great Society programs took hold.

Instead of properly identifying a cause of poverty as fatherless families, Democrats initiated programs that focused on helping unwed mothers. Incredibly, the new programs provided incentives for *more* fatherless families – not less. Then, they never repaired the programs.

Moynihan complained in the 1970s, trying to stop his party from doing the opposite of what they should do, and again, he was harshly criticized. By the end of the decade, Tip O'Neill's Congress and Jimmy Carter had cast a poverty trap for African-American mothers that locked them into the welfare state.

One such victim was Star Parker who described the experience in her book, *Uncle Sam's Plantation*. She presented her doctor confirmation of pregnancy on her visit with a welfare caseworker and describes the interview this way,

> "Let me make sure I understand you correctly. ... All I have to do for you to send me $465 per month, $176 worth of food stamps, and 100 percent free medical and dental assistance is keep this baby? As long as I don't have a bank account, or get married, I qualify for aid? Where do I sign up?"[25]

Democrats turned unwed mothering and pregnancy into a money-making enterprise. Now, it is estimated that 72% of African-American families are fatherless.

Despite that some grudgingly admitted Moynihan had been right, they still have not repaired the problem. In fact, they have increased the stipends. The twisted logic of their ideology would be better diagnosed by a psychologist, but here is a guess. It may have something to do with the idea that sending money provides salvation of guilt, or more votes, mingled with a women's liberation idea that marriage is rape and slavery.

Including all women with children (74.713 million), 15.489 million are unwed, and 30.9 percent (4.786 million) of them live in poverty; while only 6.3 percent (.976 million) of married women live in poverty. The difference indicates that if they were all married, 3.817 million women would drop off the poverty roles.[26]

But how much of this has happened since the Great Society began? Ari Fleischer cited a 2012 Heritage Foundation study saying, "In 1964 when the war on poverty began, almost everyone was born in a family

---

25 *Uncle Sam's Plantation*, by Star Parker, page 19.
26 U.S. Census Bureau, 2012.

with two married parents: only seven percent were not."[27] So seven percent of 74.713 million present-day mothers indicate that 5.223 million would be unwed, but 15.489 million are currently unwed. This is 10.268 million *additional* unwed mothers attributable to progressive policies since the Great Society began and 30.9 percent of them, 3.172 million, are living in poverty.

This is only slightly more than half of the 5.99 million seniors that would have dropped off the poverty roles had we privatized Social Security, but is clearly the second largest contributor to chronic poverty. Had progressives not created these 3.172 million impoverished mothers, the poverty rate would have dropped 8 percent.

Without the combined damage of Social Security (15%) and the destruction of marriage (8%), the poverty rate in the U.S. would have dropped at least 23 percent. Remember, the range of possible drop in poverty by privatizing Social Security was 15 to 66 percent, so the total drop of 23 percent could be much higher.

———————— ❖ ————————

Let's shift monetary incentives away from childbearing toward marriage, work, and savings. This could be phased in gently over time. Unlike some who make up the programs, these mothers are not stupid – they will follow the money.

Men cost more. Women need the monetary aid less for a baby than for a man. Consider that babies cost very little. Our lovely daughter was nursed for six months and then she ate less food in a month than I ate in one sitting. Pampers were about $40 per month. I spent that by noon. Every woman we knew within twenty klicks marched in with hand-me-downs or bought shower and birthday clothes for our daughter. When she went to high school there was a noticeable blip in cost, but not much.

---

27 Article in the Wall Street Journal, January 13, 2014.

It's the spouses that run up the bills, but a father in the home adds more earning power and much more stability in raising young men. Some men are worth the investment.

All kidding aside, how can progressives do this to women and be proud of themselves? Seventy-two percent fatherless families! Unwed mothers have enough troubles – why make poverty their home?

———•———

Let's end the insane use of food to fuel our cars. The Democrat's ethanol legislation has caused a world-wide food crisis; where in many countries, food is over 30 percent of the family budget. Hybrid electric cars are a more effective way to reduce smog. Let's stick with that.

Beef prices have increased 40 percent since the ethanol bill took effect because many beef ranchers shut down due to rising and unpredictable cost of feed. Tyson Foods and Cargill have been closing beef processing factories due to a lack of cattle. We are paying farmers to grow sugar cane to make ethanol instead of food crops. We are buying nearly half the corn crop to feed our cars. The legislation calls for even more of this insanity in the future. The price of food in the U.S. is continually rising because of this legislation. Consider the economic effect of rising food prices – it increases poverty.

———•———

Let's delete the Democrat's Health Care and Education Reconciliation Act, which they introduced two weeks after President Obama took office. The legislation kicked private lenders out of the student loan business so social engineering Democrats at Sallie Mae can provide unlimited student loans, à la Fannie Mae unlimited mortgage loans.

This allows universities to accelerate tuitions dramatically to fund staff and professor's enormous retirement pensions, with no limit except the deep pocket of taxpayers. What a scam. It could leave your children indebted for life, if they go to college, while their professors retire at age fifty-five with $120,000 per year pensions.

Previously, private banks limited loans to what they felt the student could repay. With banks out of the way, there is no cap on professorial pay, pensions, or tuitions. Under this setup, each child's debt could approach the cost of their first home. It may not matter, since such crushing debt will likely prevent them from buying a home.

There could be no better way to destroy young people's attitude toward good credit than student loan debt forgiveness, the new progressive idea: It's O.K. to borrow and not pay it back. Nevertheless, the delay of purchasing a home with a thirty year mortgage makes paying off the home a fleeting dream. This nearly eliminates the opportunity to own their home with no debt when they retire – their best chance to escape poverty.

———◆———

Let's worry about future inflation which, in the late 1970s, forced women to work. Before those three runaway inflation years, women could choose to stay home. The point to be made is not about women; the point is that, a single income was no longer enough. That inflation was caused by the explosion of government spending by the Democrat controlled congress in the 1970s, accelerated to ridiculous amounts by Tip O'Neill and Jimmy Carter.

The recent nine trillion dollar increase of fiscal and monetary stimulus is very likely to cause inflation when the economy fully recovers. What will happen to the poor if inflation lifts prices beyond their reach? Rising prices create poverty faster that any other economic event because *every* low-income individual is affected. Then we cover up the higher poverty numbers by raising the poverty level. Inflation is like the automobile accelerator of poverty.

Nearly every Democrat policy is inflationary, while nearly every Republican policy is anti-inflationary. Inflation is caused by too much money chasing too few goods. Democrat policies flood the public sector with money and produce no usable goods. Our factories produce usable goods. As we have discussed rising prices create more poor people, just the opposite effect that our factories create.

The poor have no means to protect themselves. They can't buy gold or real estate. The only economic event that causes the rich to get richer while the poor get poorer *is* inflation.

———•—•———

Let's repeal the Affordable Care Act (ACA or Obamacare). Aside from the lies about not losing your insurance or doctor, Democrats used a straw man argument to sell this legislation when they declared it was necessary to eliminate preconditions in private health policies. If individuals are allowed to demand insurance coverage *after* they become sick, the price of insurance premiums will increase dramatically. We see this happening to individual mandate Obamacare policies. For nearly a century private insurers have prevented this cheating by requiring a twelve month look back. In other words, the policy holder must make premium payments for twelve months prior to the illness. Government provided Medicaid has a three year poverty look back! So the government does this, but they won't allow evil big business to require look backs.

Elimination of the look back is the primary reason that individual mandate (families with no employer) policy premiums have increased to about 240 percent of the previous premium.[28] These are people with no employer that were required to comply with the full brunt of Obamacare on January 1, 2014.

That approximate total increase will hit employers when the employer mandate takes full effect. How many poor will be created by the layoffs?

For low-income individuals, this 240 percent increase is like their grocery store manager raising the price of bread from $2.00 to $4.80 and then

---

28 This is an estimate taken from an average of two monthly premium cases with matching deductibles: $714 to $1511, and $403 to $1,092. The lower premium of $403 is a catastrophic policy.

offering an average discount (subsidy) of 30 percent ($1.44). The optic is, "I get a 30 percent discount," but the price went from $2.00 to $3.36.

For individual mandate middle-income families making $65,000 who did not qualify for subsidies, this caused about an $8,900 per year *added expense*. The policies are not tax deductible so these couples needed a raise in income of at least $11,000 per year just to break even. Since the odds of that were nil, many moved to less expensive housing.

It is inconceivable to believe that employers will not pass most of this expense to their employees. How many of these couples will be able to afford their car(s), their apartment, or their home? They will have to move, sell and downsize. That is what we are hearing from couples who experienced the individual mandate on January 1, 2014.

Further, Obamacare copies the British system where five year fatality rates average about 20 percent higher than in the U.S.[29] Some Brits have recently warned the Obamacare elimination of doctors and hospitals for low-income Medicaid patients might increase the fatality rate up to 40 percent. So the only people to get lower insurance costs will pay with worse healthcare and a higher death rate.

The Republican's solution to rising premiums was to address the real causes. Let's allow insurance to be sold across state lines and implement tort reform. Tort reform can eliminate punitive monetary damages which punish innocent policy holders, while the guilty pay nothing. Other industries, such as real estate, have systems that punish the guilty by restriction or revocation of license to practice. Bonding and actual damages cover the aggrieved. The liberal American media and Democrats protect trial lawyers who profit by the current system. Talk about the rich getting richer and the poor (policy holders) getting poorer. Trial lawyers are highly skilled and much appreciated professionals – they can make well deserved attorney fees in order to save unnecessary expense for the innocent and low-income policy holders.

---

29 From syndicated columnist Deroy Murdock citing five year fatality rates in Great Britain 19.5 percent higher for heart attacks; and other fatality rates of 25 percent vs. 46 percent for breast cancer, 19 percent vs. 57 percent for prostrate cancer.

———•———

Let's privatize the board of directors of Fannie Mae and Freddie Mac so Democrats like Fannie Mae CEOs Franklin Raines followed by Daniel Mudd will never again social engineer mortgages for nearly anyone. These resulting toxic mortgages caused the financial crisis. This has caused all of us to suffer through the worst recession since the great depression and guess who it hurt the most? Unemployment for our fellow American African Americans rose to 15 percent and their youth unemployment to 23 percent.

———•———

In Chapter Five we noted that the poverty rate increased from 12.3 percent to 15.0 percent because of the financial crisis. It may be that there is no more important subject to understand than the true cause of our worst recession since the Great Depression. None of the books about the financial crisis has properly identified the precise cause of the crisis.

The reason these books have missed the target is that none of them are written from the perspective of, or with experience gained in, the mortgage industry. These authors tell the story from their perspective in the financial banking or securities industries. These two industries are as different from the mortgage industry as night and day, as you will learn in the next chapter where we identify the true cause of the financial crisis.

CHAPTER 7

The True Cause of the Financial Crisis

———————

Why the poverty rate rose from 12.3 percent to 15.0 percent.

A PERSISTENT MEDIA CANARD IS that the financial crisis and recession were caused by banks and Wall Street. The liberal media is covering for Democrats, who used their control of seats on the board of directors of Fannie Mae and Freddie Mac to try to create home loans for low-income families. This is noble; however as is typical, Democrats created the opposite of their intended consequences by missing the cause of the economic problem and treating it as a civil rights issue. Through their bungling, they created significant poverty and unemployment, not only here in the U.S., but throughout the world. They created the highest unemployment rate for the very people they intended to help.

There is no law against politicians and their minions making stupid economic blunders, but this may be the worst blunder ever.

The 2008 financial crisis was caused, within the mortgage industry, by Franklin Raines and Daniel Mudd (Democrat, CEO's of Fannie Mae); pushed by Andrew Cuomo (Democrat, Director of H.U.D.) and Maxine Waters (Democrat, House Financial Service Committee); and protected by financial committee chairmen Barney Frank (House Democrat) and Chris Dodd (Senate Democrat). There are other Democrats to blame, but these people made critical mistakes.

Fannie Mae and Freddie Mac, also called Government Sponsored Enterprises (GSEs), are the secondary market for all mortgages. All mortgage companies create loans using Fannie Mae or Freddie Mac loan application forms and terms so they can ultimately sell the loans to Fannie or Freddie. When Franklin Raines announced at various times that Fannie Mae would buy mortgages with credit scores below 660, and later with no income verification, the mortgage market responded immediately by beginning to produce these mortgages.

In 1992, Democrats amended the Community Reinvestment Act (CRA) to add Affordable Housing Goals for Fannie Mae and Freddie Mac. Housing and Urban Development (HUD) set the original goal. Fannie and Freddie were asked to maintain a portfolio with 30 percent of the loans to borrowers who were below the median income in the community where they live. This did not trigger Fannie's CEO to lower credit standards, but began a slippery slope of interference in the private mortgage market. HUD raised this goal to 42 percent in 1995. Still, this did not trigger Fannie to do anything wrong possibly because the then CEO of Fannie Mae refused to lower credit standards. When HUD Director Andrew Cuomo pushed the goal to 50 percent in 2000, the new CEO of Fannie Mae, Franklin Raines, began to lower minimum (FICO) credit scores which, when low enough, created toxic mortgages.

In 2000, Maxine Waters introduced the new Affordable Housing Goals to Franklin Raines before her House Financial Services Committee. At that point, Franklin Raines should have told the House Democrats, "We will do what we can, but we cannot lower income qualifying and credit standards." Instead, Franklin Raines began to lower minimum FICO scores and, later, eliminated income verification for borrowers. For example according to The Wall Street Journal, "...in each of the years 2000 and 2001, for the first time, 18 percent of Fannie's loan originations – totaling $157 billion – were loans with FICO scores of less than 660 (the federal regulators' cut-off point for defining subprime loans)." Minimum credit scores dropped steadily to 530 by 2008. A 530 FICO score is near criminal level whereby the borrower has little or no intention of paying back the loan. According to Experian data, a 530 FICO score is in the lowest five percent credit rating for all borrowers.

Franklin Raines followed, in 2004, with stated income loans – nicknamed liar loans or Alt-A loans. Stated income loans eliminated income verification, allowing buyers to enter any income they wish on the mortgage application. Making matters worse, middle-income and wealthy borrowers used stated income loans to speculate on higher priced homes in the market.

According to Edward Pinto, Fannie Mae's past chief credit officer, by 2008, Fannie Mae and Freddie Mac owned 5.7 million subprime loans (credit scores below 660) and 4.85 million Alt-A (liar loans and other junk loans) for a total of 10.55 million loans. This was 18.5 percent of all 57 million loans in the marketplace. Fannie Mae and Freddie Mac had also created millions more of these loans that they had packaged and sold to Wall Street underwriters.

Mortgage brokers create mortgages with minimum credit scores and terms set by Fannie Mae. If the loans do not meet these minimum standards, Fannie and Freddie will not buy them and the mortgage broker is stuck with loans that other investors will not buy. Thus, what Fannie says, mortgage brokers do.

In 2000 Fannie Mae signed an agreement with the country's largest loan broker, Countrywide, ostensibly to provide more of the Affordable Housing Goal loans. At that point Countrywide began sending an inordinate number of subprime and Alt-A loans to Fannie Mae to help balance their portfolio.

Mortgage banking firms act like reservoirs for mortgages between the mortgage brokers and Fannie Mae. Countrywide was both a mortgage broker and, on the back end, Countrywide Financial was a mortgage banker.

At some point, Fannie and Freddie approached their Affordable Housing Goal and both Fannie Mae and Countrywide, along with other mortgage banking firms, began to sell bundles of mortgages to Wall Street underwriters. This provided additional capital to create more of the toxic loans. Fannie Mae appears to have started this during Daniel Mudd's tenure as CEO.

Franklin Raines and Fannie Mae's subsequent CEO, Daniel Mudd, never called off the process of creating subprime and Alt-A loans, which they could have done at any time. In fact, the process accelerated.

Democrats later found it convenient to blame the mortgage crisis on the private sector, meaning Countrywide. But none of the toxic mortgages would have been created, had Franklin Raines and Daniel Mudd not allowed low credit scores and stated income (liar) loans.

WHY REPUBLICANS ARE NOT TO BLAME.

The regulator for Fannie and Freddie, the Office of Federal Housing Enterprise Oversight (OFHEO), complained from 2000 through 2006 in a series of reports to Barney Frank's House Financial Services Committee. Maxine Waters browbeat and threatened OFHEO while Republicans tried to replace OFHEO with a stronger regulator that the Democrats could not push around. Fox News reported that the Bush administration heard the complaints by Republicans on Frank's committee and "pushed Congress hard in April 2001 and again in fall of 2003 to create a new regulator that was independent from Congress." Secretary of Treasury Snow said in 2003, "We need a strong, world class, regulator to oversee the prudential operations of the GSEs [Fannie and Freddie]." Republicans on Barney Frank's committee responded with a proposed bill, HR 2575 (The Secondary Mortgage Market Enterprises Regulatory Improvement Act), to create an independent regulator.

Representative Richard Baker, Republican from Louisiana, authored the legislation. He introduced HR 2575 to Barney Frank's Committee on September 25, 2003 stating:

"Over the years, questions concerning mortgage-backed securities, leverage, capital reserve requirement, duration gap, bank investment concentration of GSE securities and a lot of other unique issues have been before this committee. I am, frankly, quite ready, in fact anxious to turn over the examination of many of these questions to a fully funded, properly constructed independent regulator, full of professionals able to give analytical examination and appropriate answers to these myriad questions. It is not business that members of Congress should routinely find themselves engaged, and I am sure many of my colleagues will enthusiastically agree with that perspective...... I look forward to making absolutely sure that the taxpayers will never be called on to pick up the tab for the failure of the system. As the Secretary has stated, Fannie and Freddie are world class financial organizations, and they require a world class regulatory structure, which is independently funded, with all appropriate authority, and the ability to make professional decisions absent political interference."

The House Financial Services Committee blocked the legislation with all Democrats voting against the Republican initiative. OFHEO did not have the power to stop the Democrats and toxic mortgages flooded the markets. Upon reading OFHEO's next report to Barney Frank's committee in 2004, Richard Baker said:

"I also wish to inform members of the Committee of another troubling incident, which I now choose to make public. About a year ago, I corresponded with the Director's [OFHEO] office making inquiry about the levels of executive compensation at the enterprise for the top twenty executives... Now I understand why the Enterprise [Fannie Mae] was so anxious not to have public disclosure of compensation of an entity that was created by the Congress, and supported by the taxpayer... As a direct result of abhorrent accounting practices, executives have been able to award themselves bonuses they did not earn and did not deserve."

Richard Baker's protestations were smothered by his House Financial Committee Chairman, Barney Frank and by Chris Dodd, Chairman of the Senate Banking Committee, who dominated the media spotlight. We did not hear about Richard Baker and the other Republicans complaints until after the crisis occurred.

The difference between banking and mortgage banking.

The media claims that banks created the mortgage loans. Banks do not create mortgages, mortgage brokerage companies do that. Wells Fargo has operated a mortgage brokerage division for years; however, they are acting as a mortgage broker and they sell the mortgages to their *non-banking* affiliates Wells Fargo Investments, LLC and Advisors, LLC (mortgage banking companies). Mortgage banking companies offer long term investments to 401(k) and other retirement programs.

Naturally there are exceptions. Indy Mac and Washington Mutual actually used bank savings deposits to make mortgages, which deposits were made whole by the FDIC when these banks failed. The way to tell if a bank made the mortgage loans is to ask, did the FDIC bail them out? The FDIC only bailed out three banks.

What of the other 511 banks that went broke? They did not originate any of the loans. The banks bought them after Fannie and Freddie sold them to the securities industry and they filtered through as AAA-Rated Bonds. The banks were the victims – not the cause.

It is important to understand that the banking and mortgage industries are different as night and day. Deposits at banks are checking and savings deposits which are the shortest of short term monies because the depositors can demand their money back at any time. That is why they are called *demand deposits*. It should be obvious that banks cannot survive using demand deposits to purchase thirty year mortgages. So how *do* banks make money?

Banks make line of credit loans (short-term money) to businesses. A typical line of credit loan of about one half million dollars will exist continuously and fluctuate up and down. The loan's purpose is to stabilize cash flow as receivables and payables ebb and flow. This assures the business they will be able to pay their suppliers and make payroll when receivables are slow. They pay the loan back down when receivables are collected. So the loan might fluctuate between about $300,000 and $400,000. The loan is short term since it is callable at any time. This matches the short term aspect of bank deposits.

Banks are required to hold a reserve requirement at 10 percent of outstanding loans. This reserve requirement money is held in the bank's securities department in the form of T-Bills and other safe securities.

Mortgages are typically 30 year loans (long-term money) and are created by mortgage brokerage companies. These companies have limited capital so they sell the mortgages to long term money investors in the secondary money market – mortgage banking firms. The mortgage banking firms hold some mortgages for investment and resell the rest to Fannie and Freddie.

Mortgage banking firms are not nearly large enough to provide capital for the entire mortgage industry. Fannie and Freddie hold the vast majority of mortgages.

Since banks do not want to tie up capital in long term money, life insurance companies were the secondary money market for mortgages after World War II. Even life insurance companies could not provide enough capital for the post war housing boom, so Fannie Mae and Freddie Mac became the secondary money market for mortgages. These corporations are traded on the stock exchanges which provide capital from investors worldwide. The money does not come from banks.

Occasionally during boom times, Fannie and Freddie have run low on capital to buy mortgages and would bundle mortgages and sell them to Wall Street underwriters, such as Goldman Sachs and Lehman Brothers, etc. The underwriters can make any number of investment products out of the mortgages such as mortgage backed bonds and then submit that product to Moody's Investor Service for a rating prior to sale.

WHY FANNIE MAE IS TO BLAME.

The obvious reason that Fannie is to blame is that only Fannie Mae sets minimum FICO scores. Remember, this was called the "subprime crisis." A subprime loan is a loan with a FICO score below 660. Fannie Mae also dictates the other loan criteria, so they are entirely to blame. The CEO of Fannie Mae acts like a fleet captain for Fannie and Freddie, so the blame centers on the Fannie Mae CEO, and no one else.

Experts from the financial industry, who have little understanding of the mortgage industry, incorrectly assign blame to other factors. Most of these false theories developed on financial industry news shows and were perpetuated by the rest of the media. This could be called the CNBC explanation.

Democrats and Independents run to Factcheck.org, which is really just an extension of the New York Times and other leftist news networks. On Factcheck.org, Joe Miller blamed everything *except* Fannie and Freddie. This includes the bubble theory, the low interest rate theory, and the low down payment theory. None of these had anything to do with the crisis.

The bubble was about the same size as the previous three bubbles. Here are values that can be proven from a tract of homes named College Park in Costa Mesa, California. A three bedroom 1,850 square foot home was worth about $45,000 in 1974. That same home doubled in early 1976 to $90,000 (100 percent increase). It doubled again during the inflation years 1978-1980 to $180,000 (100 percent increase). It doubled again in 1989 to $360,000 (100 percent increase). Leading up to this crisis from 2000 to 2008, it only slightly more than doubled to $750,000 (110 percent increase). The bubble was not the cause of the crisis.

With regard to low interest rates, we had low interest rates throughout the 1950s up to 1976 and they did not cause bubbles or financial crashes.

Low down payments had nothing to do with the crisis. FHA's west coast regional manager, Charles Ludlam in 2010, stunned a California audience with the statement that, "A year and one-half after the crisis began, while delinquency rates of mortgages at Fannie and Freddie had risen to 26 percent, delinquency rates at FHA [3.5 percent down payments] had only risen to about 8 percent."

The chart at the end of this chapter is the author's effort to test his statement and also determine the timing of the toxic mortgages. The delinquency rates shown are from the Mortgage Bankers Association website and verify his claim that, "Low down payments had nothing to do with the crisis."

Notice the 7.96 percent delinquency rate includes VA loans which are zero percent down payment! Ludlam queried, "Does anyone know why our [FHA] delinquency rates did not rise [like Fannie and Freddie]? No one raised their hand. "It's because we never stopped qualifying income and we did not lower FICO score requirements."

Further proof that Fannie Mae is to blame.

Understanding discount points is critical to understanding why Fannie Mae, not mortgage bankers and mortgage brokers, caused of the financial crisis.

Home buyers pay a discount point with their closing costs. A point is one percent of the loan amount ($1,000 for a $100,000 loan). This is to reimburse the mortgage banking firm for discounting the loan when they sell it to Fannie Mae. Fannie Mae's standard discount is one point for loans that meet their lending standards such as FICO credit score and income qualifying standards. If the loan meets these standards, Fannie will pay $99,000 for a $100,000 loan. This, in effect, is a guarantee of 99 percent of the loan.

Without this guarantee, discounts on custom mortgages between buyers and sellers in the open investor market typically vary from 20 percent to 50 percent. In other words, a $100,000 loan would resell for $50,000 to $80,000; a $20,000 to $50,000 loss.

Why the large 20 percent to 50 percent discount? It costs a lot to take back and resell a house. Consider this: The loss of payments during the foreclosure period of 6 months for trust deeds and 2 years for mortgages may cost, say, 5 percent of the loan amount. Fix-up costs of around $30,000 may cost, say, 10 percent, and commission and escrow fees may cost 8 percent of the loan amount. This adds up to a 23 percent loss on the loan. In recent years, these mortgages have been selling for about a 55 percent discount because low appraisals and dropping prices also add to lender fears.

No mortgage banking firm or mortgage brokerage company would dare make a loan that does not meet Fannie Mae's credit and qualifying standards because they need the 99 percent guarantee. Non-qualified loans are occasionally created by seller carry back financing and, if sold, sell for the deep discounts mentioned.

As a result, mortgage brokers will only lend within Fannie Mae's credit and qualifying standards. What Fannie says, mortgage brokers do. Owners of these qualified loans know they can sell them to Fannie Mae for 99 cents on the dollar. This creates an open market for mortgage banking firms to buy and sell loans that are supported in value by Fannie Mae.

When Fannie Mae announced they would buy loans with FICO scores down to 650 (10 points below prime, meaning subprime), they opened a large new market of borrowers who had not previously qualified for loans. Even though the loans should have been worth less because of the low credit score of the borrower, the loans were effectively guaranteed by Fannie Mae and Moody's ultimately rated them AAA.

Banks eventually began to buy them as investments for their securities department reserves. *That* is how the banks ended up with the loans. They did not make the loans – they bought them after Fannie and Freddie created them.

Fannie Mae could have stopped these low credit score loans from being produced immediately by announcing they would no longer buy them. Instead, they called for lower and lower credit scores all the way down to FICO scores of 530. If Fannie Mae didn't call for them, the loans never would have been produced.

Only Fannie Mae sets the minimum FICO scores. When Fannie Mae announced each new lower minimum FICO score, mortgage brokers and most real estate agents quickly called potential clients who could not previously qualify.

In retrospect, according to Edward Pinto's numbers, each time Fannie Mae announced a ten point drop in the minimum FICO score, they created about 1.25 million new subprime loans.

Fannie Mae made so many of these loans that they began to run short of capital. Leading up to the crisis, to provide additional capital, Fannie Mae began to bundle mortgages and sell them to Wall Street. Some mortgage banking firms did the same. So long as the terms of their mortgages matched Fannie Mae requirements, they were marketable.

Thanks to Franklin Raines touting the mortgages as safe and the assumption that the government (Fannie Mae) stood behind them, the mortgages became security for AAA- Rated Bonds as they bled through Wall Street to the securities departments of banks.

Franklin Raines said in 2004, "These assets are so riskless that the capital for holding them should be under two percent." That would have been an egregious violation of law for any other CEO.

HOW DID THIS AFFECT THE BANKS AND WHAT WAS TARP ABOUT?

The mortgage bonds replaced safe securities and shrank the bank's required ten percent reserves when the mortgage bonds were later devalued. The low reserves required the bail out so banks would not have to call loans to businesses. This would have been an economic catastrophe whereby many businesses, having their line of credit cut back, might not be able to make payroll.

The first half of TARP ($330 billion of $700 billion) prevented the catastrophe by purchasing bank stock, providing the necessary bank reserves that had shrunk due to the near worthless mortgage bonds. This money was eventually paid back by banks buying back the stock from the government. The tax payers actually made money because the banks bought their stock back at a higher price.

President Bush ended the program in December, 2008 saying, "It worked." He was right, the deep crisis had been averted and there was no more need to pump money into bank reserves. The second half of TARP ($370 billion) was later restarted in 2009 and wasted trying to lower interest rates by purchasing treasury bonds from banks.

———◆———

If toxic candy is produced in bulk (by Franklin Raines and Daniel Mudd, Fannie Mae CEO's) and placed on a street corner, we should not blame the people who become sick or die from eating it (Wall Street and the banks).

It has been estimated, within the mortgage industry, that the average down payment from 2000 to 2008 was only about six percent for purchase money (non-refinance) loans. So the homeowners lost 6 percent and must regroup by renting for two to five years before they can again qualify for a loan. Home values fell about 35 percent; therefore, banks lost about 29 percent. To date, over 511 banks have closed.

The largest percentage losers were the shareholders of Fannie and Freddie, whose stock plunged from over $60 to 25 cents per share.

We need Fannie and Freddie. Without them, home loans would become scarce and extremely expensive (remember the 25 to 50 percent open market discount).

Currently, we are doing the worst thing possible. We are funding Fannie and Freddie with our tax dollars because investors have no interest in the stock. Under Barney Frank and Chris Dodd's inept leadership, American taxpayers funded about $169 billion in just the first three years to support operations at Fannie and Freddie.

This taxpayer funding could grow dramatically as the economy recovers while private investors are unwilling to fund the GSEs. Currently home sales are about a fourth of what they will be in a healthy market; so ultimately, taxpayer funding could balloon to near $200 billion per year. We need to create shareholder confidence to attract private capital back into the GSEs (Fannie and Freddie).

Barney Frank and Chris Dodd do not seem to care and may leave the GSEs as nationalized corporations – or worse, as they have discussed, eliminate the institutions entirely. They seem happy to have skimmed

$239 billion in profits from Fannie and Freddie. Now they have another nationalized cash cow in addition to our Social Security.

In early 2005, having been accused of accounting fraud by OFHEO for apparently removing cash from capital reserve accounts to create "profits" and resulting bonuses for the directors of Fannie Mae, Franklin Raines finally relinquished control of the GSEs. Daniel Mudd, another Democrat and son of TV anchor Roger Mudd, replaced Franklin Raines and accelerated the same destructive practices until the collapse of the markets. On September 7, 2008 Mudd was fired by the federal conservator that was charged with managing the insolvent GSEs.

WHAT SHOULD BE DONE?

Barney Frank and Chris Dodd should be ousted from their positions on financial committees. An independent regulator should be created for Fannie Mae and Freddie Mac. HR 2575 should be reintroduced and passed.

Fannie Mae and Freddie Mac should be chartered to buy prime mortgages at a one percent discount, but no longer run by Democrats while their stock is traded on a stock exchange. The board of directors of both corporations should be privatized.

Mortgage industry experts who know what they are doing, not Democrat social engineers, would be appointed to the board of directors. The directors would answer to an independent regulator staffed with mortgage experts, and answer to the shareholders who would insist that the directors create investment quality mortgages that are safe for investors and for homeowners.

THE FINANCIAL CRISIS INQUIRY COMMISSION AND HOW DEMOCRATS USED IT TO WIN THE 2012 ELECTION.

In 2010, Democrats set up a commission to analyze what went wrong. Phil Angelides, Democrat and past California Treasury Secretary, was named chairman of the Financial Crisis Inquiry Commission (FCIC). In 2011, Angelides summarized that the private sector was at fault. The

FCIC reported that they tested "a subset of borrower's loans...by the end of 2008...and far fewer GSE mortgages were seriously delinquent than non-GSE mortgages: 6.2 percent versus 28.3 percent." In other words, Fannie did not create *any* bad mortgages.

What "subset" Phil? That 6.2 percent is similar to the 7.22 percent FHA/VA delinquency rate over at Ginnie Mae where they had not lowered credit and qualifying standards. Did you use those loans as a subset?

Are we to believe that Fannie and Freddie's subprime and Alt-A loans were only 6.2 percent delinquent while everyone else's subprime and Alt-A loans were 28.3 percent delinquent? Did you use Fannie's prime loans as a subset, because that was the delinquency rate of prime loans?

Phil Angelides was telling us not only that Fannie Mae did not create any bad loans, but they didn't even own any. According to Edward Pinto's data, that is as obviously false as an employee with red sunburn trying to convince his boss he was really out sick the day before. As mentioned, Edward Pinto's statement and data shows that Fannie and Freddie were caught red-handed with 10.55 million subprime and Alt-A liar loans in September 2008.

The evidence that Fannie Mae called for and bought these loans is overwhelming. Yet, this is the canard that the Democrats used to win the 2012 election and the lie that our dishonest liberal media perpetuates, including Wikipedia.

Peter J. Wallison, apparently the only conservative on the commission, wrote a scathing dissent to the FCIC conclusion. Wallison later reported that past Fannie Mae Chief Credit Officer Edward Pinto, offered a "70 page, fully sourced memorandum" which was ignored by the commission. Commission member, Peter Wallison, stated in the American Spectator,

> "This information, [Pinto's memorandum] which highlighted the role of government policy in fostering the creation of these low quality mortgages, raised important questions about whether the mortgage meltdown would have been so destructive if those policies had not existed. Any objective investigation would have looked carefully at Pinto's research, exposed it to the members

of the commission, taken Pinto's testimony, and tested the accuracy of his research. But the commission took none of these steps. Pinto's memos were never made available to other members of the FCIC...Philip Angelides would not allow the staff to pursue any theories about the causes of the financial crisis other than those embodied in the standard left-wing narrative."

Daniel Mudd, CEO of Fannie after Franklin Raines, claimed (paraphrasing), that at Fannie Mae we never lowered our standards – the private market did that. Why did you buy them then? How then, did you end up with so many subprime and Alt-A mortgages? Why then, are your loans performing so poorly if they are all prime mortgages? Why then, seven years later, was your $60 per share Fannie Mae stock (FNMA) still selling for only 35 cents?

Michael Bourne of U.S. News and World Report quoted Barney Frank's committee member Democrat Representative Artur Davis saying,

"Like a lot of my Democrat colleagues, I was too slow to appreciate the recklessness of Fannie and Freddie. I defended their efforts to encourage affordable homeownership when, in retrospect, I should have heeded the concerns raised by their regulator in 2004. Frankly, I wish my Democrat colleagues would admit, when it comes to Fannie and Freddie, we were wrong."

REGARDING THE NEXT PAGE:

Following is a one page chart of the author's backup data accumulated from searching actual mortgage broker files to determine when each type of toxic loan first occurred.

This identifies, by date, which CEO of Fannie Mae first allowed each type of toxic mortgage. Franklin Raines (1999-2005) was the first to allow all four toxic loan types.

Also listed are the delinquency rates to determine whether low down payment loans were a part of the cause. It proves that low down payments did not cause the crisis.

REGARDING THE FOLLOWING PAGE:

This is a chart from Edward Pinto's report that was ignored by Phil Angelides and kept from FCIC commission members. The chart was an internal company memo to employees of Fannie Mae and Freddie Mac warning about FICO scores below their own self imposed limit of 660. Note that it is dated 1995, before the first subprime loans.

The chart proves that it was common knowledge at Fannie and Freddie that lowering credit standards below 660 FICO scores would create high delinquency rates for loans. It proves Franklin Raines and Daniel Mudd knew that damage would be caused to the banks that purchased the loans and to their own shareholders – they simply did not care.

LOW DOWN PAYMENT LOANS DID NOT CAUSE THE FINANCIAL CRISIS.

DELINQUENCY RATES

MINIMUM FICO SCORES

YEAR	VA 0% DOWN	FHA 3.5% DOWN	SUB-PRIME (CREDIT SCORES BELOW 660) AND STATED INCOME DELINQUENT RT	STATED INCOME (INCOME NOT VERIFIED) FICO's	SUB-PRIME (INCOME VERIFIED) FICO's
2000					650
2001					640
2002					625
2003					610
2004				750	590
2005				725	575
2006				700	560
MAR 2007	6.49%		13.77%	675	545
JUNE 2007	6.15%		14.82%	650	545
DEC 2007	6.49%		17.31%	640	545
MAR 2008	7.22%		18.79%	630	530
DEC 2008	7.52%		21.88%	n/a	n/a
MAR 2009	8.21%		24.95%	-	660
MAR 2010	7.96%		25.69%	-	630

Source: Mortgage Banker's Association, (MBA).

Source: Estimates from American Financial Network.

ATTACHMENT 2

Industry Letter

July 11, 1995

Freddie Mac

SUBJECT: The Predictive Power of Selected Credit Scores

TO: CEOs and Credit Officers of all Freddie Mac Sellers and Servicers

Having bought over 16 million loans during our 25-year history, Freddie Mac is in a unique position to conduct research and spot industry-wide trends. Sharing observations about industry trends and offering tools to help you manage the mortgage lending process are key ways we fulfill our mission of making decent, accessible housing a reality.

We recognize the challenges of today's market environment. To assist you in meeting these challenges, we want to provide you tools to underwrite credit risk and meet the needs of every creditworthy borrower. One such tool is the use of certain credit scores to help you focus your underwriting efforts.

Research Findings

Freddie Mac studied how hundreds of thousands of loans performed over several years to determine which attributes of the loan file were most predictive of default. We identified a strong correlation between mortgage performance and two types of credit scores, created by national credit scoring companies and frequently used in consumer lending. The types of credit scores we reviewed were "bureau scores," as prepared by Fair, Isaac and Co., Inc. ("FICO") and "bankruptcy scores," as prepared by CCN-MDS ("MDS"). The chart below illustrates the predictive power of these credit scores.

Predictive Power of Credit Scores

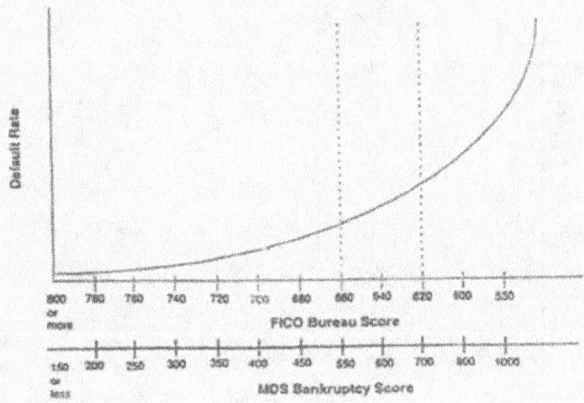

CHAPTER 8

What Franklin Raines Should Have Done

———◆———

How to help minorities buy homes.

In 2000, MAXINE WATERS INTRODUCED the new Affordable Housing Goals to Fannie Mae requesting more loans for low-income households. At that point Franklin Raines should have said, "We will do what we can, but we cannot lower loan qualifying and credit standards." So what *should* Franklin Raines have done? Here is one idea.

He should have said, "We will promote home ownership in low-income neighborhoods by target marketing. The program might be called, *Income Growth and Home Ownership.*

First, the program would provide motivational advertising explaining how people become wealthy through home ownership. Television ads would give real life examples about young minority couples. If Maxine Waters could arrange federal tax credits to the television stations, the ads would cost the program almost nothing. This would make possible ongoing advertising.

Second, the program should provide goals by explaining the various affordable down payments. VA loans are available to veterans with as little as no down payment. FHA insured loans are available to anyone with down payments as low as 3 ½ percent. Conventional loans are available at 5 percent down with the payment of Private Mortgage Insurance (PMI).

It should be noted that the financial crisis damage was not caused by low down payments. It was caused by "stated income" loans (called liar loans because income was not verified) and lowering of credit standards to below 660. In June 2010, a year and one-half into the crisis, conventional loan default rates (60 days late) had risen to 28 percent. FHA insured loan default rates had only risen from about 6 percent to 7 ½ percent.

The FHA west coast regional manager, Charles Ludlam, explained why, "We never stopped verifying income or lowered our qualifying formulas or our credit [FICO score] standards." Real estate agents generally claim the part of the market that recovers fastest is the low price market driven by young couples using FHA loans. So the pundits who say that only large down payments will solve our problems are wrong.

Third, the program would explain the income required to get started. This would be roughly $70,000 per year in many neighborhoods of an inner city for a two bedroom condominium, with two people earning $35,000 each. Jobs that pay this amount or more might be: A good waiter/waitress at a restaurant or a restaurant manager; salesperson; truck owner operator; UPS driver; construction worker; government jobs, etc.

Fourth, the program advertisement would encourage a single person to not wait. Find a friend who also makes this much and buy a home together. It should tell them, "You may find that your incomes and your equity will grow within a few years. At that point, you can sell to buy for yourselves, or you can rent the condo to others. Guess what? You are now landlords."

Also, this is their sole and separate property. This is a legal term that means that if they marry, they cannot lose the equity in a divorce. This might ring a bell for young men. Further, a single male homeowner will find more ladies willing to date him.

For young women, it is empowering. If a single woman homeowner marries someone who cannot afford the area, he will not need to take her out of the county to purchase housing. Since she already owns a home, they can stay close to her family. Parents appreciate this as well.

The program should give real life examples. Had Franklin Raines done this, we would not have toxic mortgages.

The program could be funded by a Fannie Mae sponsored foundation that would include promotional information and donation requests to Fannie Mae shareholders in their annual prospectus mailing. The foundation should also advertise for donations nationwide. Of course, Mrs. Waters might promote a little government sponsorship.

CHAPTER 9

The Imminent Explosion of Economic Problems

The Supreme Court is out of their league.

REPUBLICANS RESOUNDINGLY WON THE 2010 midterm elections by blaming Barney Frank as the banking queen; a snide political quip, but very effective. Later, during the 2012 election campaign, Republicans were confronted with the Phil Angelides lie.

They did not know enough to refute it so they gave in and took the blame for the entire financial crisis in this simple exchange: President Obama declared, "I inherited this financial crisis and recession." Republicans replied, "Yes, but you have had three years to fix it."

That was an admission that the financial crisis was the Republican's fault!

Independents, Asians and many others were natural to think, "See, the Democrats must be right. Republicans don't deny that the financial crisis was their fault. Let's do what President Obama asks and give him more time to fix it. Obama is right, employment is rising and our 401(k)s are booming, so what he is doing must be working, although slowly, so he needs more time."

Republicans need to study to win elections. The reason is that Democrats are venturing into management of a very complex world – the private sector. Had Republicans understood the true cause of the financial crisis, they would not have made the aforementioned mistake.

Republicans are not alone. All politicians and judges, including the Supreme Court, are out of their league in understanding the consequences of the Democrat's foray into private sector management.

THE SUPREME COURT IS OUT OF THEIR LEAGUE.

When liberal Justices of the Supreme Court approved Obamacare, they authorized an average 240 percent increase in premiums for victims of the individual mandate (people with no employer), and later for victims of the employer mandate.

For employers of middle-income families making $65,000, who do not qualify for subsidies, this will cause about an $8,900 per year added expense. How many of these couples will lose their job, their hours worked, their apartment, their car, or their home? How many will divorce to qualify for subsidies when they get sick?

Liberal Justices on the Supreme Court allowed Democrats the authority to remove doctors and hospitals from Medicaid, which the Brits warned will decrease the survival rate of the poor. They gave Democrats the right to restrict return visits to the hospital for the same malady, restricting our right of survival. They gave one Democrat the power to do "as the Secretary determines," without higher authority. In other words, they have given Democrats nearly complete control of our medical industry – and our survival.

When the Supreme Court allowed the EPA to regulate the use of carbon dioxide, they approved an 83 percent reduction in the use of clean burning natural gas at our utilities and factories. The 75 percent reduction imposed by the original cap-and-trade rule in the Los Angeles basin caused two thirds of the factories to close and is the reason we are now buying so much from China.

The Democrat's planned 83 percent reduction will close thousands of factories nationwide. Already the EPA is implementing, in pieces, the outline of HR 2454, which the Republicans had wisely voted down in the Senate.

Yes, the rule is spread out over thirty-eight years and it regulates use of 25,000 tons per year, which seems like a high threshold; but as we witnessed in Los Angeles, the Democrats will reimpose the rule at lower and lower thresholds. This will affect smaller factories and they will close throughout the term of the rule. It should not be imposed on *any* factories, or utilities, no matter their size.

The Supreme Court does not understand that carbon dioxide does not cause warming. Nor do they seem to understand that warming, if and when it happens, is healthier for us. One does not need to be a scientist to recognize this. Consider the number of species of animals that thrive in the warmer climate of the equator. The number of species decreases as they live further away from the equator to almost zero at the poles. This is true in the plant kingdom as well.

The Supreme Court allowing Democrats to manage medicine, science, technology, and economies in the private sector is like allowing a four-year-old to fly the Space Shuttle.

If the Constitution truly allows all this, it needs to be amended. In the meantime, if the Supreme Court is going to allow Democrats to abandon laissez-faire, it would be helpful to study these issues, or demand proof, to better understand consequences of the decisions.

ACADEMIA IS OUT OF THEIR LEAGUE AS WELL.

Academia is out of their league with respect to regulation of carbon dioxide. As mentioned, this writer owned a company that performed gas physics training, Weights and Measures testing, instrument repair, and solved real world gas physics problems throughout the southwestern United States. We were thrown into the fire of learning the most complex gas physics challenges of our time. We were the first to determine how to measure drifting landfill gas; digester gas at sanitation plants; biogas at food processing plants; and flare gas out of the stacks at oil refineries. These solutions are well beyond what universities teach or understand.

Academia teaches the theoretical physics of thermodynamics, some of which has proven to be false and cannot be used to solve real world problems. Thermodynamics lays as a foundation using two theoretical forms of energy: internal energy and the infinity of potential energy. There are no engineering charts or conversion tables for them, since they are only theoretical.

The theory's inference that the *only* way something cools is to radiate heat away has been proven false. Temperature, for the most part, cools in place. The implication was that heat energy simply goes elsewhere and cannot be destroyed, which is also false.

Temperature is simply the measurement of force caused by the speed that atoms and molecules are moving. For example, consider what happens when photons from the Sun hit mercury in a thermometer. The mercury atoms accelerate, colliding with each other and with the glass wall. The increased force causes mercury to rise in the thermometer. When the Sun goes down, the mercury slows. Any small amount of temperature that radiates to (collides with) nearby molecules also slows and stops. Temperature does not go anywhere; it simply slows, and if cold enough, the material freezes.

Academia teaches formulas such as Boyles Law and other formulas that do not work. Over a century ago, Rockwell and American Meter engineers determined that Boyle's Law does not work. Engineers have replaced Boyles Law with a calculus they call supercompressibility, and the calculus changes with the type of instrument used to measure the gas.[30]

Gas physics in the private sector has advanced far beyond these 100 to 350 hundred year old gas physics theories. Real world gas physics (outside of academia) is created and taught by engineers at our factories that manufacture gas instruments and equipment. The equipment *has* to work or the engineers lose their jobs when customers complain, equipment catches

---

30 Boyles Law is PV=K. It was postulated by Professor Robert Boyle in 1662. It describes the expansion and contraction of gas with a change in pressure. Private sector engineers now use multiple calculus formulas called supercompressibility that they determine by such testing as U.S. Patent No. 4584868.

fire, or pipelines explode. Academia can be wrong without consequence. The private sector cannot survive by using misinformation.

Academics (political activists as pointed out in Chapter Two) dredged up the old greenhouse theory to justify regulating carbon dioxide. John Tyndall's experiment and thirty-six page paper, written in 1861, is the much referenced scientific study behind the greenhouse theory and global warming.

No new significant science has been added to the greenhouse theory since the paper was written. Advocates even use Tyndall's exact words from the paper. Some further studies have chopped temperature into various wavelengths to overanalyze the subject, but it is still just temperature.

John Tyndall spent two years building a large device (*Figure 1*) that uses a galvanometer to measure gas temperature. It did not quantify temperature. It measured only the movement of a gauge with gradation marks. To make a thirty-six page paper short, Tyndall proved, generally, that the larger the molecule, the more heat it absorbs. His results are listed on page thirty-one of his paper.[31]

Tyndall lists air as absorbing "0" temperature; then in increasing numbers, carbonic oxide, carbonic acid, nitrous oxide, and olefiant gas. Olefiant gas is ethylene, which is the largest molecule in the group. Air is a *mixture* of two unconnected atoms: oxygen and nitrogen. *Compound* molecules are connected atoms, such as CO_2. Tyndall's results show, *mixtures* such as air (N & O) do not absorb as much temperature as compound molecules. He never tested carbon dioxide. It likely would have absorbed temperature near the lower end of this group, since CO_2 is a small compound molecule.

At this point he ended his good science of measuring relative temperature absorption to surmise what is now the greenhouse theory: Since air absorbs almost no temperature it is, in Tyndall's words, "transparent to the rays of the sun" which penetrate the air to warm the earth's surface, (these are some words advocates still use today). Some temperature that is

---

31 Published in *Philosophical Transactions*; Titled, *On the Absorption and Radiation of Heat by Gases and Vapours.*

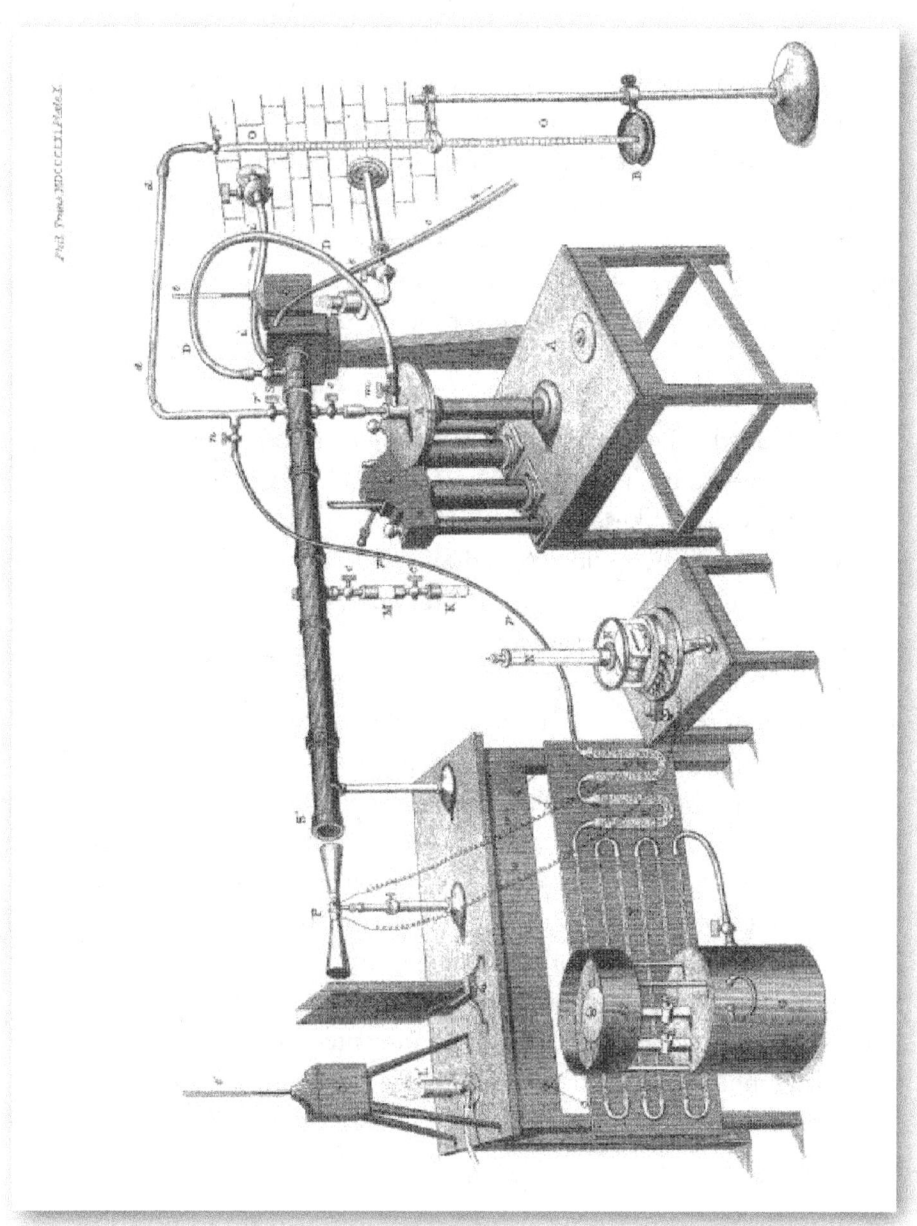

Figure 1

absorbed by earth is radiated back up and such small amount of temperature is absorbed by compound gases (greenhouse gases in today's jargon).

This sounds good, but Tyndall's conclusion that air in the atmosphere absorbs almost no temperature is wrong. It absorbs an average of twenty-two degrees Fahrenheit every sunny day. Obviously, he was wrong because he was measuring temperature below the accuracy range of his instrument. He was using a candle flame as a heat source. The instrument did not accurately measure at that low temperature.

Further, when he *did* obtain readings, his indicator needle wagged like a compass. On page two, he made his first attempt to mitigate this saying, "I therefore sought to replace the Berlin coil with a less magnetic one." So the galvanometer that he had purchased was no longer calibrated for accuracy.

We never would have put our weights and measures sticker on John Tyndall's device for these and several other reasons.

More important, Tyndall's study was half complete. The study lacks the essential element of time. How long do any of these compound gases retain the absorbed temperature?

Tyndall's assumption that the atmosphere retains heat because compound molecules absorb more heat than air is like saying an automobile engine accumulates heat over time because the pistons absorb more heat than the distributor cap. Does your engine accumulate heat over time? Does anything accumulate heat over time because one part absorbs more heat than its other parts? The answer is no. Tyndall's conclusion is invalid and wrong. Why Tyndall sensationalized is for others to speculate, but he did sensationalize.

Today, in climate controlled proving rooms, we test and calibrate many instruments that measure temperature. Modern volume correctors (computers) data log changes in temperature instantaneously. These devices are far more sophisticated than John Tyndall's galvanometer. Our experience with this allows us to witness that gas temperature changes *very rapidly*.

THE CORRECT SCIENCE.

John Tyndall's testing was half finished. He did not time how long these gases retain the temperature. Tyndall's good findings were that gases cool in proportion to the amount of temperature they absorb and vaporous gases absorb about 13 times more temperature than dry gases. The combustion process creates dry carbon dioxide.

This experiment should be conducted on pure carbon dioxide, which would require some limited funding. Lacking such funding, we conducted a test on vaporous (70 percent humidity) atmospheric air including carbon dioxide therein. The air-carbon dioxide mixture was isolated in an air tight, insulated test room and heated. Once the heat source was discontinued, temperature dropped steadily at about 1 degree Fahrenheit every 32 minutes. Using Tyndall's finding, we divide 32 minutes by 13 to estimate that dry air and carbon dioxide cool each degree in about 2 ½ minutes.

Since carbon dioxide from combustion is always dry, this is a fair marker for the length of time it would take for it to lose any gained temperature once the heat source is removed. During a typical sunny day, our atmosphere absorbs about 22 F. *The dry carbon dioxide, cooling each degree every 2 ½ minutes, would lose all that temperature in about 55 minutes. This cooling is faster than the 24 hours required to create a greenhouse effect.*

Even the vaporous mixture cools faster than 24 hours. That is why Monday might be colder than Sunday. Temperature does not and cannot accumulate in our atmosphere.

Yes, some gases absorb more temperature than others; but, for how long do any of them retain that temperature after the heat source is removed? The answer is, for minutes, and certainly not the twenty-four hours required for the greenhouse theory to be true.

In other words, carbon dioxide is not a greenhouse gas. That is the real reason it does not cause warming – it cools too quickly. Only in academia are there greenhouse gases. In the real world, they don't exist.

A number of scientists have offered proof that carbon dioxide does not historically comport with temperature and further, that it is beneficial, not harmful. Nearly half the nation is aware that the claims of the global warming activist professors are false. Congress voted their proposal down.

Why would the Supreme Court allow these political activists to regulate carbon dioxide based on false claims without proof?

Perhaps the Supreme Court should have required proof (a test) to prove that carbon dioxide retains heat for at least twenty-four hours before accepting the declaration that it causes warming. Simply run carbon dioxide through a coalescing filter, at low pressure, into any aluminum or stainless steel container and warm it 20 degrees. Any container will slow the cooling process. Time how long it takes to lose that temperature. It is a simple test – measure it.

THE IMMINENT EXPLOSION OF ECONOMIC PROBLEMS.

Throughout our history, Democrats have confined themselves to fiscal issues such as budgeting, tax rates, and statutes that protect the public from harm or fraud. They practiced laissez-faire policy guided by our Constitution.

When Democrats implemented the RECLAIM rule in Los Angeles, it marked a turning point whereby they set up an agency with no oversight by Congress or legislature, and it could write any law it wanted. What followed was a series of inane laws that forced our factories to close.

When Franklin Raines lowered the government's minimum FICO score below 660 in 2000, it marked an exit from government guidance and an intrusion into management of the private sector. What followed was the worst recession since the Great Depression. For Democrats, there was profit in the ensuing confusion.

When President Obama decided to take profits from Fannie and Freddie rather than payback by company dividends, he nationalized the mortgage industry. Just as they do with our Social Security pension money, from now on, they will skim profits off the top. As of October 2015 they had skimmed $239 billion of Fannie and Freddie's profits, far more than the government invested.[32] Think they will stop? No, they simply move on to the next industry to nationalize and skim profits.

---

32 *Wall Street Journal*, by Joe Light, October 20, 2015.

When Democrats passed Obamacare, they proclaimed that the Secretary of Health and Human Services, one Democrat, would effectively run the medical industry. The economic destruction has already begun. We are stuck with regulation of doctors and hospitals that limit care for the poor, nearly triple the cost of insurance premiums for middle-income families and, you guessed it, more revenues for the government.

Now that Democrats have abandoned laissez-faire and are venturing into hands-on private sector control, Republicans need to learn how to solve the upcoming explosion of complex economic problems – just like any CEO. The old approach of simply lowering taxes won't be enough. The Supreme Court, however they do it, should end the creation of politically autonomous agencies that are set up to run the private sector.

We are in a new time when fiscal and monetary polices will not fix the economic problems that Democrats are causing. We have entered a time of economic destruction.

CHAPTER 10

Where the Democratic Party Went Wrong

Why they chose socialism and how their media became dishonest.

As with any economic problem, finding and repairing the root cause is critical to a solution. Sometimes management is the problem.

We cannot fire a political party. Nor do we wish to eliminate the good that resides in the Democratic Party – a desire to help the poor. However, if we are going to help Democrats attain this exceptional goal, we must be honest about what they are doing wrong.

We need a rational and well informed Democratic Party in the United States. A socialist government however, only creates more of the poor who they claim to help. Furthermore, our leftist media has become dishonest and lies to Democrats to prevent conservative solutions.

The original Democratic Party that protected states' rights and cared for the individual has been damaged by these two wrong turns: socialism and media dishonesty.

DEMOCRATS DID NOT START AS SOCIALISTS.

The Democratic Party began with a healthy respect for states' rights and individual rights. That was excellent, except that they also began with a terrible ball and chain – slavery and racism. This left northern Democrats with a significant feeling of guilt, which led to their choice of socialism.

The Democratic Party was founded by Thomas Jefferson, who was a southern plantation owner that owned one hundred forty slaves at one time and over six hundred in his lifetime. Shocking but true, Thomas Jefferson once pointed out that his slaves provided a four percent profit simply by the birth of their children. He later claimed that slaves should, in addition to crops, "bring a silent profit of from 5 to 10 percent in this country by the increase in their value."[33]

Slavery was *condoned* by the founder of the Democratic Party. The Whig Party opposed slavery. Naturally, most southerners followed Jefferson's lead and became Democrats. They claimed to need slavery and profited by it. In effect, slaves became a part of their GDP (Gross Domestic Product). Historian David Brion Davis said, "In 1860, the value of southern slaves was about three times the amount invested in manufacturing or railroads nationwide."[34]

State law dictated each state's status as a Free State or Slave State. All of the southern states (south of the Mason-Dixon Line, Pennsylvania's southern border, and below the Ohio River) made slavery legal. Southern Whigs, like Abraham Lincoln's father, migrated to northern Free States.

By 1854, northern Whigs had generally confronted the dwindling number of southern Whigs to either give up slavery or they were not Whigs. Finally, the few remaining Whigs in the South folded in with the Democratic Party. The southern Whig Party disappeared. *The South became essentially all Democrats with a unified cause – slavery.*

Later that year, Abraham Lincoln, led by others, broke away from the Whig Party to form the Republican Party. Although Whigs wanted to end slavery, some wanted to appease the South and did not want to give African

---

33 *Smithsonian Magazine*; October 2012, by historian Henry Wiencek, pages 42-44. This part of our history was generally sequestered until recently when Jefferson's entire life-long *Farm Book* journal of operations was made available to historians. Henry Wiencek is one or those historians.

34 Ibid.

Americans the right to vote. Lincoln and the rest of the Republicans felt that African Americans should have *all* rights offered to others.

Subsequently, in the Civil War, about 160,000 Republicans died – fighting Democrats – to end slavery.[35]

In 1865, after the war ended, President Lincoln gave a speech encouraging voters in Louisiana to confer the voting franchise to African Americans in their new constitution. John Wilkes Booth was in the audience and his co-conspirators testified at their trial declaring, *that* was the reason Booth killed Lincoln.

So, our first Republican president ended slavery and died trying to obtain voting rights for African Americans. The next Republican president, Ulysses S. Grant, finished the job Lincoln had started, winning the right to vote for African Americans in 1870.

In 1866, six southern Democrats founded the Ku Klux Klan (KKK). Confederate war veteran Democrats, Major James R. Crowe (no relation to Jim Crow laws), Captain John C. Lester, Calvin Jones, Richard Reed, John D. Kennedy, and Frank McCord formed the KKK.[36] Their expressed purpose was to, "Keep [African Americans] in their place and continue to fight radical Republican policies." Thereafter, southern Democrats perpetuated the KKK and racism for nearly one hundred years.

African Americans, nationwide, commonly voted for Republicans.

Eighty-two years later the issue of racism by Democrats came to a head again. At the 1948 Democratic Convention, Hubert Humphries introduced a civil rights platform and began a campaign to end racism *within his own Democratic Party* in the South.

He declared, "My friends, to those who say that we are rushing this issue of civil rights, I say to them we are 172 years late. To those who say that this civil rights program is an infringement on states' rights, I say

---

35 An estimate extrapolated from the percent of Republicans in the 1860 election and the number of northerners killed in the war.

36 State Senator Stephen Martin referring to founders of the KKK, "It wasn't an official subdivision of the [Democratic] party, obviously, but it was definitely was founded by Democrats." Such was also told by a number of southern historians.

this: The time has arrived in America for the Democratic Party to get out of the shadow of states' rights and to walk forthrightly into the bright sunshine of human rights."

Southern Democrats formed the Dixiecrats to oppose him.

After battling Dixie*crats* (all Demo*crats*) for sixteen years, Humphries, with significant help from Martin Luther King, finally won the Civil Rights legislation battle in 1964.

Humphries did not write the Civil Rights Act of 1964, nor did other Democrats. It was essentially copied from the Civil Rights Act of 1875, which was written by Republicans, and beaten back by Democrats. The 1875 bill, authored by Senator Charles Sumner (R-MA), passed but was immediately challenged in court by Democrats. The suits were eventually combined into one case that won in the Supreme Court in 1883. The court ruled that Lincoln's 13th Amendment did not extend to private individuals or organizations, only to the states. The lone dissent on the court was by Republican Justice John Harlan. Defeat of the Republican's Civil Rights Act of 1875 opened the door to our nation's ugly history of segregation.

Prior to our left-wing media's subsequent dishonest campaign to flip-flop the truth, which began in the 1960s, African Americans voted consistently for Republicans. Even today, when asked to name an elected Republican racist, Democrats can't do it.

They point to David Duke and Republicans agree, he was most definitely a racist (and a con-man); but he was a Democrat. He rose through the ranks of the KKK to become Grand Wizard, as a Democrat. He later ran in four elections, including a presidential primary, as a Democrat. In 1988, he changed parties to run in a special election against John Treen because he knew he could beat him. Treen had previously suggested raising property taxes. Duke hammered away at this statement and won. When Duke arrived in Congress, Republicans were not familiar with him because he had been in their party for a brief time. When Democrats pointed to him as a racist, Republicans were appalled. Unlike the Democrats, Republicans ostracized Duke. In 1990, Republican Party Chairman Jim Nicholson stated, "There is no room in the party of Lincoln for a Klansman like David Duke."

And no, Strom Thurman was a Dixiecrat – a Democrat. He changed parties in 1965, declaring that he wanted to join the party that had been right all along.

Note that a number of Klansmen have been successful in the Democratic Party, including Bull Connor (police commissioner), Lester Maddox (governor), George Wallace (governor, and presidential candidate), Robert Bird (speaker of the house) and, although briefly, Harry Truman (President). No Klansman has ever succeeded in the Republican Party. The Party won't allow it and their voters won't allow it.

Robert Byrd, Democratic Speaker of the House, was a Grand Kleagle in the KKK. Byrd was elected in 1952 and *continuously re-elected, by Democrats*, for his entire career until his passing in 2010.

Democrats allow their media to lie to them, blaming others for racism. They can argue with this and nitpick the details, but they need to stop blaming others for racism and slavery when it was their own southern Democrats that were the sole purveyors of that terrible history. It also, may have led their party into socialism.

In the 1840s, northern Democrats had sympathized with southern Democrat slave owners, declaring that slavery was necessary to support the southern economy.

There is significant evidence that northern Democrats were racist as well – voting nearly unanimously against Lincoln's first attempt to pass the 13th Amendment to end slavery. However, there is also evidence that they at least felt guilty. They occasionally dubbed themselves Conscience Democrats.

In 1848, Karl Marx published the *Communist Manifesto* and some of the Marx/Engels socialist essays. U.S. newspapers discussed them extensively. Many northern Democrats pounced on the opportunity to assuage their guilt. Newspaper publishers led the way. Throughout the 1850s, while the tension over slavery grew, the media and Democrats became economic liberals.

Many in the media such as Horace Greeley became self avowed socialists; but at least up until 1974, the media was honest.

How and when the media became dishonest.

Most will admit that Democrats and Republicans are on nearly opposite sides of many issues. The reason is that the Democrat media leads Democrats to nearly the opposite of the truth on almost any politicized subject:

Republicans are racist; no, it has been just the opposite.

Global Warming is bad for us; no, if and when it is happening, it is good for us.

Science is on our side; no, it is on the side of the global warming deniers.

Banks caused the financial crisis; no, they were the victims and 511 of them closed.

Big business is evil; no, they have been the creators of wealth and reduced poverty.

Social Security is saving our seniors; no, it is locking them into or near poverty.

This is an extremely serious problem. If we don't repair it, our economy will slowly deteriorate and poverty will continue to be an unsolvable problem.

Polar opposite viewpoints did not exist before 1974. Democrats were statesmanlike and truthful. They would not have vilified Reagan or Bush. They offered rational ideas of how to improve our society. They were able to recognize the cause of our problems. Insightful Democrat leaders like Hubert Humphries and Daniel Patrick Moynihan were not alone. Then, the media changed and Democrats followed.

In 1973, Woodward and Bernstein became media heroes. Their investigative reporting of Watergate was envied by editors and lead reporters nationwide. There is nothing wrong with investigative reporting, that is what reporters should do.

What went wrong started with the television news show, *60 Minutes* with Dan Rather. The war had ended and leftist concern shifted to the environment. *60 Minutes* produced investigative journalist reports about large corporations polluting the environment. Generally, *the 60 Minutes stories were created with a predetermined outcome.* Sound familiar? Ideologues cannot solve economic problems because they predetermine who is to blame, which means they miss the true cause of the problem.

60 Minutes became the most popular news show on television. All the news services followed their lead. Editors would call journalists into their office and say, "Go get a story on that chemical company that is dumping chemicals in the river." With this new approach, the outcome of *the story was presumed and predetermined.* This is the primary characteristic contributing to media dishonesty.

Chemical factories are not much more than a blending process where liquids are brought in by rail, blended, and sold in barrels. The various liquids are pumped from rail cars into large polymer or stainless steel tanks inside the factory. The liquids are then batched (pumped and measured) into blending tanks and then into barrels ready for shipment. There is no waste. The amounts not used remain in the inventory tanks.

Factory employees would comment on the media attacks about their industry by explaining that chemical companies do not dump chemicals, they sell them.

Imagine an investigative journalist confronting an executive with the accusation that he is dumping chemicals in the river. It is likely the executive would walk that journalist through the entire factory and explain their process.

Most journalists would go back to their editor and say, "There is no story here." Apparently the editor would say, "Oh come on, if you can't handle this, I will get someone who can." In this way, the honest reporters were shuffled to other stories and the lead stories were given to reporters willing to cut and paste interviews to match the predetermined outcome. This was the critical reason and time that the media became dishonest. But the story goes on.

In 1975, the media blamed the entire oil crisis on our oil companies. Republicans blamed OPEC. When the second oil crisis hit in 1978, I became insatiably curious and could not stand the finger pointing and confusion. I decided to conduct my own research.

The Los Angeles Times was perniciously blaming the oil companies. In all the articles that I clipped over the next year, there was enough supply data to assemble a crude understanding of who was exporting to us and how much. Our own domestic production was published each week in the Los Angeles Times Sunday business section. This number was provided by the oil industry and hovered at 10 million barrels per day of domestic production.

It took about a year to assemble all of the supply data and determine our imports to be roughly 7 million barrels per day. Demand was fluctuating around 17 million barrels, equaling maximum supply. I learned by reading industry publications that our oil companies purchased from the exporting nations in layered contracts.

For instance, if an oil company felt they would need 1 million barrels per day, they might purchase 500,000 barrels per day at $8.00 per barrel for 10 years; 300,000 barrels per day at $10.00 per barrel for 5 years; 100,000 barrels per day at $12.00 per barrel for two years; 50,000 barrels per day in one year contracts for $13.00 per barrel and the remaining fluctuating amount of roughly 50,000 barrels per day would be purchased on the spot market for a higher price.

The spot price might range from $13.00 to $20.00 per barrel depending upon demand of the various oil companies. It was this spot market price that we saw in the newspaper every day.

The truth of what happened was this: In 1970, the price of oil was about $1.25 per barrel. Our demand was high and increasing. OPEC exporters were matching the demand, though they were nearing their export capacity.

In May 1970, a bulldozer broke a pipeline near the Persian Gulf and the spot market price of oil doubled until the pipeline was repaired. Muammar al-Qaddafi of Libya noticed this and called Armand Hammer of Occidental Oil for a meeting. Qaddafi imposed a tax that matched the spot market price increase and Occidental's cost tripled.

Armand Hammer emerged from that meeting saying, "The western world will never be the same again." The other OPEC members began imposing taxes. During the first oil crisis in 1976, OPEC members imposed an approximate average $6.00 tax taking oil to about $8.00. During the second crisis in 1978, they imposed another tax of about $5.00 taking the price to about $13.00 per barrel.

It took about a year and one-half of homework and research to determine all this. The difficulty in finding the truth was frustrating. I lost all trust in the Los Angeles Times and other news organizations; most of whom used a predetermined outcome for their stories that our oil companies were to blame.

Not one news organization reported the truth about either energy crisis, not one. This is a second characteristic necessary to understanding the new media. When it comes to a story that the media wants to predetermine, *the media flies in a single flock*. Notice how they interview each other for these stories. Media hosts would interview other media members such as correspondents and bureau chiefs who reflect the flock mentality. They never interviewed Armand Hammer.

Bernard Goldberg, who quit CBS News to report on media bias, wrote a book named *Arrogance*. He explained this flock mentality by essentially saying that television news people wake up in the morning and read the New York Times trying to decide which will be their lead story of the day. They call each other to pin down the choice.

For example, when a newspaper reporter coined the term Star Wars for Ronald Reagan's SDI proposal, Dan Rather squawked, "Star Wars" and the entire media began squawking, "Star Wars" like a flock of parrots.

Subsequently, a third pillar of media dishonesty arose. In 1978, CBS reporter Tritia Toyota stuck a microphone in a nine year old girl's face and asked, "Aren't you afraid that your next president might start a nuclear war?" The media's attack on Ronald Reagan began and did not stop until 1990, two years after he left office.

By this time the media's two tactics were apparent; to predetermine the outcome of certain stories, and to fly in a single flock parroting the story. But the media pounced on the opposite side of every one of Reagan's proposals and later they did the same to President George W. Bush.

This brings us to a third observation necessary to determining truth in today's world. The media was not simply anti-Reagan, they were anti-Republican. They had become activist *anti-Republican and anti-big business.* These are the two templates through which all news must pass before it reaches us.

Some very dramatic news events that did not fit through these templates have not reached us, even to this day. For example, President Clinton turned down extradition of Osama bin-Laden. That is a big story. Bill Clinton admitted this claiming essentially that we did not have the evidence to convict him and yet, reporters will not report it.

When Democrats are out of power, the media becomes activist in their opposition to anything Republicans propose or try to accomplish; hence, the polar opposite points of view.

The left-wing media pounds canards into Democrat's heads: Republicans are stupid rubes, unfeeling, uncaring, fascists, homophobes, and of course, racists. The left-wing media divides us by economy; by rich, by middle class, by poor. They divide us by race; by white, by black, by brown, by the Rainbow Coalition. They divide us by gender; by sex, by same-sex, and by Republicans versus women.

So, what do Republicans really think? They think, "Stop trying to divide us with class warfare – we are all Americans. Compassion should be measured, not by the number of people receiving welfare, but by the number no longer needing it. Let's fix our economic problems so all of us will benefit."

CHAPTER 11

Why Socialism Creates Poverty

———

How we can support the poor without destroying the economy.

THE SOVIET UNION AND CHINA proved that elimination of capitalists created poverty for all. The United States confirmed that truth in the obverse by allowing the genius of our factory owners to create wealth for all.

Socialism survives on the noble ideal to help the poor, but operates with a false economic assumption made a part of the philosophy by Karl Marx. He said, "The abolition of bourgeois individuality, bourgeois independence, and bourgeois freedom is undoubtedly aimed at."[37] In other words, in economic terms, the wealthy harm or stand in the way of the poor. This is the false and destructive aspect of the socialist economic philosophy.

An evolution of how this philosophy spread has become apparent. The leadership becomes implacable because they are convinced they are morally correct to help the poor.

In dictatorships, such as the Soviet Union, the philosophy was forced upon the media. We labeled the philosophy's false notions as propaganda and used Radio Free Europe to send truth to Soviet citizens.

---

37 *The Communist Manifesto*; by Karl Marx and Frederick Engels, International Publishers, page 24.

In democracies, the media becomes the implacable leader. Each time a conservative leader tries to solve economic problems, the media seeks to destroy the leader. Another socialist is elected and the economy spirals further toward shortages and poverty.

Socialist economics are only half right. Supporting the poor is the good and necessary half. The destructive and unnecessary half seeks to revile and destroy the people that create wealth. This socialist revulsion extends to what they might call the entire capitalist complex. Unfortunately, it is an unbending ideal that limits their understanding and makes them implacable.

There is nothing wrong with Democrats on the street, except that they believe their media which continuously lies to them. Because they are ideologues, they believe only what fits into their ideology. The leftist media knows this and feeds them any absurd information that the media thinks might further the cause of destroying Republicans and the capitalist complex (big business).

The point was made earlier that, becoming liberal is an epiphany, becoming conservative is a learning process. The epiphany is, "I care about the poor and want to help them. I want to help our minority fellow Americans rise from their economic malaise." This is perfect – keep it – but they should begin the learning process.

Fortunately nowadays there is an alternative, truthful media. Conservatives hear both media sources. We can't help listening to the leftist media. It rains down on all of us from newspapers, magazines, television, movies, everywhere. We make the effort to listen to conservative talk radio. Nearly half the nation does this. Liberals are trained by the leftist media to revile and hate conservative talk radio. Listening won't kill them – and it will start a learning process that is surprising to liberals when they experience it.

One misconception, molded by the leftist media, is that liberals are more intelligent. The thought is that liberal leaders are so intelligent, how can they be wrong? There are intelligent people on both sides. The problem is that intelligent people on the left absorb the media-fed misinformation faster and remember more of it. For this reason, intelligent Democrats are actually *more* misinformed than other Democrats.

Another implacable misconception is that Republicans don't care about the poor and minorities. Not only do Republicans care, but they have excellent ideas of how to repair the economic malaise of the poor. The leftist media won't listen, much less learn.

———◆———

In these chapters, we have examined the destructive and unnecessary policies that are creating poverty in America.

It is unnecessary and destructive to impose cap-and-trade regulations on factories that cause them to close. Factories create wealth and reduce poverty by making high volumes of usable goods at affordable prices.

It is unnecessary and destructive to impose carbon dioxide limits on electric utilities, which drive up utility bills. Consider who that hurts the most – the poor.

It is unnecessary and destructive to allocate healthcare based on income up to $65,000 per year. Obamacare, by its design, is already drawing middle-income people into lower incomes in exchange for healthcare. It is also causing employers to lower incomes by changing workers to part-time pay.

It is unnecessary and destructive to spend over twice the cost of the Iraq War every year (the stimulus), for no effective reason. This floods the public sector with money and produces no usable goods. This will eventually raise prices and therefore, poverty. The poor have no defense for inflation and it affects *all* low-income people.

It is unnecessary and destructive to nationalize the mortgage industry so progressives can try again to help the poor, only to send them deeper into poverty in an ensuing financial crisis. When mortgages are given to people who cannot pay them back, there will be a crisis. Unemployment follows.

It is unnecessary and destructive to nationalize the student loan business, only to create a generation of youth that begins life mired in debt.

It is unnecessary and destructive to use food to fuel our cars, only to create more poverty by raising food prices.

It is unnecessary and destructive to tax our factories at the highest rate in the world, only to chase them out of the country; thus, reversing the engine that drew millions out of poverty.

It is unnecessary and destructive to incentivize mothers to not work, not to save, not to marry and, instead, to have babies. These inane programs have caused poverty to rise by eight percent.

Democrats wonder why the poverty rate has not gone down. *Stop causing it to go up.* Clearly the most effective way to start is to allow 83 percent of all Americans, in the private sector, to keep and own their pension money. Privatize it. The leftist media has tried to make privatize a taboo word. Good economic ideas can't be talked into becoming bad ideas.

The charts in Chapter Four prove that our poverty rate would have dropped by at least 15 percent and the Chileans proved that there are three additional ways privatization can reduce the poverty rate up to 66 percent. This one simple correction would reduce our poverty rate somewhere between 15 and 66 percent.

It is unnecessary and destructive to take 15.3 percent of a citizen's taxable income every year and then pay them back a median pension that is below poverty level for an elderly couple.

Exhibit 2 in Chapter Four, at the bottom of the column showing lifelong income, shows the average taxable annual income of an individual necessary to have become a millionaire. At the current tax rate of 15.3 percent, that average annual taxable income is $19,846. To the right is their accumulated private savings of $1,002,937.

Think about that. That average taxable income is $9.54 per hour. Such a worker would have become a millionaire had we privatized Social Security.

Think about what we will be doing for our impoverished fellow Americans who feel they have no hope of success. That $9.54 per hour is near entry level pay anywhere in our three-tier-distribution system. As they work, they will watch their pensions grow at a miraculous rate. They will become millionaires; if not, they will be close to it.

If we simply privatize Social Security – *that* would create a realistic road to wealth for the very poor who need it the most. The poor will not only have a ladder out of poverty, they will have a catapult to wealth.

Acknowledgements

———————

CREDIT IS OWED TO INDIVIDUALS from my two careers in the private sector, where true economic and scientific learning begins.

My first career, in real estate, began by knocking on doors, then some mortgage brokerage, and then into industrial real estate in downtown Los Angeles with The Seeley Company. Roy Seeley founded the company in 1908 with broker number 00000008, the eighth license in the State of California. At Seeley Company, I was trained by my mentor, Tom Taylor, and by Bill Renwick. Thank you both. I eventually found success by specializing in the relocation of factories.

I fancy that, not only is relocating factories the most complex of real estate transactions, it may be the most complex of all business transactions. These transactions involve hundreds of laws, rules, codes, approvals, and regulations that consume about five years from bare land to finished factory.

It was here and on my hundreds of factory tours that I observed that all wealth is created by factories.

While at Seeley Company, a client offered to sell his business to me. It was, among other things, a distributorship of gas physics instruments. The distribution aspect of the business and the experience with factories made clear my understanding of what made America so wealthy. To write about that subject in Chapter One, I required help from a business historian, Harold Lovesay. His book, *American Made* answered my most important question, "Who invented the distribution system?"

My company included another division, which was a California Weights and Measures test and repair facility for industrial applications. The other, state owned, Weights and Measures test laboratories only handled gas pump and residential submetering. We were nearly overwhelmed with the myriad of complex industrial testing.

I thank Ron Brown, who ran that division. My partner called him a self-taught genius, and an executive from Schlumberger told me he thought Ron was the best test and repair technician in the country. Ron was faced with a daily deluge of gas physics instruments, both mechanical and computer operated, which were sent to him for test and repair.

My other manager, of operations, was Tim Wetzel. Tim was the sole source, throughout the southwestern U.S., to call for help in solving commercial and industrial gas physics problems. His ability to solve these daily complex problems over the phone was extremely impressive.

Both of my managers helped me to learn gas physics. They also sent me into the field to solve complex problems that required on site inspection. Nearly all of our employees became experts in gas physics.

Thanks to Bob Bennett, who is the North American gas physics trainer for American Meter Company. He originally trained me, and my employees. His company invented the first gas measurement instrument in 1836. Its design is still in use today, in front of your home.

Index

www.ingramcontent.com/pod-product-compliance
Lightning Source LLC
Chambersburg PA
CBHW072206280526
45788CB00002B/897